Morality, Ethics and Responsibility in Organization and Management

In the aftermath of the financial crisis, and regular corporate scandals, there has been a growing concern with the moral and ethical foundations of business. Often these concerns are limited to narrow accounts of governance codes, regulatory procedures or behaviour incentives, which are often characterized by neoliberal bias underpinned by western masculine logics. This book challenges these limited accounts of ethics and responsibility.

It looks at the writing of Gayatri C. Spivak who takes globally networked markets, people and ideas and provides tools to rethink subjectivity, ethics and corporate governance. Eschewing strict hierarchical notions of authority and identity, Spivak's work invites us to consider who speaks for whom and for what in organizational contexts. Relationality is also to be found in the radical politics and feminist ethics of Judith Butler who continues to draw on and develop her account of performativity to interpret contemporary organizations, management and work.

While popular accounts of corporate ethics often concern themselves with the aims and actions of those at the top of organizations, Lauren Berlant focuses on the struggles of those at the bottom of the new social structures created by contemporary forms of capital. Finally, the book also considers ecological challenges through the work of Val Plumwood, who spent a lifetime considering the threats and responsibilities we face in environmental terms, and developed a feminist ecological philosophy for understanding social and species differences.

This book will be relevant to students and researchers across business and management, organizational studies, critical management studies, gender studies and sociology.

Robert McMurray is Professor of Work and Organization at The York Management School, UK.

Alison Pullen is Professor of Management and Organization Studies at Macquarie Business School, Sydney, Australia.

Routledge Focus on Women Writers in Organization Studies
Edited by Robert McMurray and Alison Pullen

Given that women and men have always engaged in and thought about organizing, why is it that core management texts are dominated by the writing of men? This series redresses the neglect of women in organization thought and practice and highlights their contributions. Through a selection of carefully curated short-form books, it covers major themes such as structure, rationality, managing, leading, culture, power, ethics, diversity and sustainability; and also attends to contemporary debates surrounding performativity, the body, emotion, materiality and post-coloniality. Individually, each book provides stand-alone coverage of a key sub-area within organization studies, with a contextual series introduction written by the editors. Collectively, the titles in the series give a global overview of how women have shaped organizational thought.

Routledge Focus on Women Writers in Organization Studies will be relevant to students and researchers across business and management, organizational studies, critical management studies, gender studies and sociology.

Gender, Embodiment and Fluidity in Organization and Management
Edited by Robert McMurray and Alison Pullen

Rethinking Culture, Organization and Management
Edited by Robert McMurray and Alison Pullen

Morality, Ethics and Responsibility in Organization and Management
Edited by Robert McMurray and Alison Pullen

For more information about this series, please visit: www.routledge.com/Routledge-Focus-on-Women-Writers-in-Organization-Studies/book-series/RFWWOS

Morality, Ethics and Responsibility in Organization and Management

Edited by
Robert McMurray and Alison Pullen

Routledge
Taylor & Francis Group

LONDON AND NEW YORK

First published 2020
by Routledge
2 Park Square, Milton Park, Abingdon, Oxon OX14 4RN

and by Routledge
605 Third Avenue, New York, NY 10017

Routledge is an imprint of the Taylor & Francis Group, an informa business

British Library Cataloguing-in-Publication Data
A catalogue record for this book is available from the British Library

Library of Congress Cataloging-in-Publication Data
Names: McMurray, Robert, 1972- editor. | Linstead, Alison, 1971- editor.
Title: Morality, ethics and responsibility in organization and management / edited by Robert McMurray and Alison Pullen.
Description: Abingdon, Oxon; New York, NY: Routledge, 2020. | Series: Routledge focus on women writers in organization studies | Includes bibliographical references and index. |
Identifiers: LCCN 2020001519 (print) | LCCN 2020001520 (ebook) | ISBN 9780367234140 (hardback) | ISBN 9780367234133 (ebook)
Subjects: LCSH: Business ethics. | Social responsibility of business. | Management—Moral and ethical aspects. | Organizational sociology.
Classification: LCC HF5387 .M6543 2020 (print) | LCC HF5387 (ebook) | DDC 174/.4—dc23
LC record available at https://lccn.loc.gov/2020001519
LC ebook record available at https://lccn.loc.gov/2020001520

ISBN 13: 978-0-367-23414-0 (hbk)

Typeset in Times New Roman
by codeMantra

Contents

Series note

This series arose from the question: given that women and men have always engaged in, and thought about, organizing, why are core management texts dominated by the writing of men? Relatedly, and centrally to the development of organization studies as a field, the following questions rose: Why do so few women theorists and writers appear in our lectures and classes on managing, organizing and working? Why has the contribution of women to organization theory been neglected, indeed, written out of, the everyday conversations of the academy?

This series redresses the neglect of women in organization thought and practice. It does so by highlighting the unique contributions of women in respect of fundamental organizational issues such as structure, rationality, managing, leading, culture, power, ethics, diversity and sustainability, while also attending to more nuanced organizational concerns arising from issues such as performativity, the body, emotion, materiality and post-coloniality.

Through a selection of carefully curated short-form books, the series provides an overview of how women have shaped organizational thought. This series is international in scope, drawing on ideas, concepts, experiences and writing from across Europe, North America, and Australasia, and spanning more than 150 years. As the series develops our ambition is to move beyond even these confines to encompass the work of women from all parts of the globe.

This is not a standard textbook. It does not offer a chronological history of women in organization theory. It does not (cannot) claim to be the complete or the last word on women in organization: the contribution of women to organization theory and practice continues and grows. We do not even promise that each chapter will be written like the one that preceded it! Why? It is because the variation in style and substance of each chapter deliberately reflects the varied, exciting and often transgressive women discussed. Indeed, one of the points of this series is to draw attention to the possibility that there are as many ways of thinking about, writing on and doing organizing as there are people. If you want to read and think differently about management, work and organization then this is the series for you.

Readers of this and other volumes in the series will note that the first person is often employed in our accounts of women writers. Reference is made to meetings with writers, to the personal impact of their thinking and to the ways in which writers have moved or challenged their researches personally. Once again, this personal emotional approach to assessing the work of others is at odds with more positivistic or masculine approaches that contend that the researcher or analyst of organizations is to remain outside, beyond or above the subject matter: an expert eye whose authorial tone allows them to act as dispassionate judge on the work of others. We argue that the fallacy of neutrality that results from such masculine positivism hides the arbitrary and inherently biased nature of subject selection, appraisal and writing. Just as importantly, it tends to produce sterile prose that does little to convey the excitement and dynamism of the ideas being discussed.

The subject matter of this book has been chosen because the chapter creators believe them to be important, and thought has been given to the selection of the women writers shared with you. Authors recognize the bias inherent in any writing project; it is writ-large in the title *Focus on Women Writers* and is more explicit in some chapters than others. In editing this series, we have been struck with the enthusiasm that informs how our authors have chosen influential women writers, and this enthusiasm can be read in the ways in which the chapters engage with the work of specific writers, the application of these writers to organization studies and the personal reflections of the influence of writers on their own research. The perspective from which we – and our authors – write is therefore open for you (the reader) to read, acknowledge and account for in the multiple ways intended. The lack of consistency with which the authors address fundamental organizational issues should not be read as lacking rigour, but rather bring an alternative way of leveraging critical thinking through an engaged, personal approach to the field. In this way, authors embody the ideas and ethos of the women writers chosen. While written in an accessible form, each chapter is based on years of engagement with the works of women writers and an in-depth appreciation of their contribution to and impact on organization studies. There is also critique. The omissions or controversies that have accompanied the work of these writers are addressed, along with challenges to their work.

The result is a collection of books on *Women Writers* that are scholarly, readable and engaging. They introduce you to some of the most important concepts in organization studies and from some of the best theorists in the field. Politically and ethically we hope that this book will help students, lecturers and practitioners reverse a trend that has seen women writers written out of organization theory. Just as importantly, the inclusion of such work usefully challenges many long-held beliefs within mainstream management literature. We hope that this series will be the beginning of your own personal journey of ideas – the text and suggested readings produced in this book offering starting point for your own discoveries.

Routledge Focus on Women Writers in Organization Studies will be relevant to students, teachers and researchers across business and management, organizational studies, critical management studies, gender studies and sociology.

Contributors

Agnes Bolsø is Professor of Gender Studies at Norwegian University of Science and Technology. Her main research interests are connected to gender, sexuality and power, empirically explored in a variety of cultural, social and organizational contexts over the years. She is recently the co-editor of *Bodies, Symbols and Organizational Practice* (Routledge, 2018).

Department of Interdisciplinary Studies of Culture,
Norwegian University of Science and Technology,
Norway.agnes.bolso@ntnu.no

Barbara Czarniawska is Professor of Management Studies at Gothenburg Research Institute, University of Gothenburg, Sweden. She takes a feminist and processual perspective on organizing, recently exploring connections between popular culture and practice of management and the robotization of work. She is interested in in techniques of fieldwork and in the application of narratology to organization studies.

GRI, School of Business, Economics and Law,
University of Gothenburg,
Barbara.czarniawska@gri.gu.se

Nancy Harding is Professor of Human Resource Management at the University of Bath School of Management. Her research interests are 'working lives', or more specifically in asking 'what is it like to be this person doing this job in this way at this time and in this place?' Her previous book projects include two sole-authored books, the first *The Social Construction of Management* exploring the manager (Routledge, 2003), the second *On Being at Work: The Social Construction of the Employee* (Routledge, 2013), with a third, 'the organization', planned but severely delayed. Her joint-authored books include Fotaki and Harding's (2017) *Gender and the Organization: Women at Work in the 21st century* on feminism, and Ford,

Harding and Learmonth's (2008) *Leadership as Identity: Constructions and Deconstructions.* She also co-authored a book *The Social Construction of Dementia: Confused Professionals?* (Harding and Palfrey, 1997).

University of Bath School of Management.
h.n.harding@bath.ac.uk

Kate Kenny is Professor of Business and Society at NUI Galway, Ireland. Her research focuses on identity, affect, power and whistleblowing in organizations. Kate's work has been published in *Organization Studies, Organization, Gender Work and Organization, ephemera* and *Human Relations,* among other journals. Books include *Understanding Identity and Organizations* (Sage, 2011, with A. Whittle and H. Willmott), *Affect at Work: The Psychosocial and Organization Studies* (Palgrave, 2014, with M. Fotaki), *Whistleblowing: Toward a New Theory* (Harvard University Press, 2019) and *The Whistleblowing Guide* (Wiley Business, 2019, with W. Vandekerckhove and M. Fotaki).

School of Business and Economics and
Whitaker Institute, NUI Galway, Ireland.
Kate.kenny@nuigalway.ie

Robert McMurray is Professor of Work and Organisation at The York Management School, UK. Research interests include the organization of health care, professions, emotion labour, dirty work and visual methods. Other collaborative book projects include *The Dark Side of Emotional Labour* (Routledge), *The Management of Wicked Problems in Health and Social Care* (Routledge) and *Urban Portraits.*

The York Management School,
University of York, UK.
robert.mcmurray@york.ac.uk

Banu Özkazanç-Pan, PhD, is Professor of Practice at Brown University's School of Engineering and School of Professional Studies. She is the Co-chair for the Academy of Management Diversity and Inclusion Theme Committee and Past Co-chair of the Critical Studies Management Division. Banu is the Joint Editor-in-Chief of Gender, Work and Organization. Her research interests include leading for diversity and inclusion in organizations and entrepreneurial ecosystems, examining the future of work and its impact on different people, organizations and societies and studying the intersections of culture, post-coloniality and transnationalism as they relate to changing nature of work and societies. Recently, she was asked to testify at the US Senate Committee on Small Business and Entrepreneurship to speak about the importance of women and minority investors and entrepreneurs. She is the co-editor of three books including the *Routledge Companion to Gender, Work and Organization* and the author of *Transnational Migration and the New Subjects of Work: Transmigrants, Hybrids and Cosmopolitans* (Bristol University, 2019). Her most recent book, *Entrepreneurial Ecosystems: A Gender Perspective* (Cambridge University Press, 2020), will examine the rise of ecosystems from a critical gender framework.

Brown University's School of Engineering and School of Professional Studies.
Banu_Ozkazanc-Pan@brown.edu

Alison Pullen is Professor of Management and Organization Studies at Macquarie University, Australia and Editor-in-Chief of *Gender, Work and Organization*. Alison's research has been concerned with analyzing and intervening in the politics of work as it concerns gender discrimination, identity politics and organizational injustice.

Macquarie University, Australia.
Alison.Pullen@mq.edu.au

1 Introduction

Morality, ethics and responsibility in organization and management

Robert McMurray and Alison Pullen

Concern with the moral and ethical foundations of business have long remained a social and political question. Ethics is often positioned as some sort of antidote to the reckless and self-interested behaviour that too often characterizes business activity. Ethical attention is thus directed towards the complex and rampant profiteering that led to the Global Financial Crisis of 2008, as well as myriad corporate scandals ranging from the Union Carbide Bhopal gas leak disaster in 1984, the Enron accounting scandal in 2001, British Petroleum's culpability on the *Deepwater Horizon* oil spill in 2009, the News International phone hacking fiasco in 2011 and the Volkswagen emissions scandal in 2015. Often responsibility for ethics in business is limited to practice such as corporate social responsibility reporting, ethical codes, regulatory procedures or behavioural incentives. Even where well meant, it is evident that such approaches speak to particular western masculine logics of a neo-liberal variety – logics that often fail to account for the interconnected and interdependent nature of businesses, peoples, species and environments, or for the growing social, political and economic power of corporations. While the Global Financial Crisis saw banks fail, homes repossessed and entire countries brought to their knees, its aftermath brought an austerity-based fiscal policy and a populist political ideology to the fore in too many countries. In this dire context, the need of alternative thinking when it comes to business and management ethics is palpable.

In this, the fifth book in the *Focus on Women Writers in Organization Studies* series, a range of different approaches to understanding the place and responsibilities of organizations and their actors are offered. Underpinning much of what follows is a nuanced consideration of how (and by whom) our knowledge and associated histories are constructed. This is important in so far as it determines who is heard, who is acknowledged, who is attended to and whose needs are prioritized. The result is a series of chapters that point to the rejection of Cartesian mind–body split while eschewing the normative prescriptions associated with codes and procedures. In its place there is an emphasis on the value of inter-disciplinarity, recognizing our connections, accounting for context, giving voice to those who are unheard or silenced and recognizing that managing and organizing are part of the wider world rather than detached, external and neutral.

Together, the writers of the chapters featured in this book take us beyond what others see as the greenwash of corporate social responsibility (CSR) reports and the platitudes of ethical codes so as to think more deeply about the nature of morality, ethics and responsibility in organization studies. On that basis, this is a book for students, managers and citizens who have observed that traditional corporate approaches to ethics are not working and want to understand why and what might be done otherwise.

We open with Barbara Czarniawska's chapter on the life and work of Maria Ossowska. As with other contributions to this series, the chapter invites us to reconsider our taken-for-granted assumptions on the nature of reality, knowledge and morality and, in particular, a strongly western masculine tendency to see progress as a linear journey driven by intellectual giants. Czarniawska's chapter draws on a process of re-remembering in relation to the life and work of Maria Ossowska. This personal account invites us to consider what it means to take part in the 'conversation of science'. Specifically, the idea that science reflects a linear progress, based on the brilliance of intellectual giants who proclaim their own worth, is quietly unpicked as we trace the course of Ossowka's academic development. A wide-ranging career is described as informing contemporary themes in organization studies including morality, studies of science and technology (SST), feminism, philosophy, method and popular culture. It is notable that Maria Ossowka's work was not limited to or by disciplinary strictures but, quite the reverse, sought to move across such boundaries so as to avoid unreflective reasoning. Maria Ossowska offers texts that are readable and questioning. Barbara Czarniawska concludes that Ossowska offers students of organization studies two key lessons. First, a transdisciplinary approach is essential to understanding the complex phenomenon that is organizing. Second, the style of our writing is important if it is to be read. There is then no moral prescription or ethical formula offered here for the reader. Rather, we are sensitized to the possibility that knowing, acknowledging, relating and reflecting are themselves ethical acts.

In Chapter 3 Agnes Bolsø takes up the baton of considering the relationship between science, morals and organizing, this time in respect of the environment. While there is a broad scientific consensus that global warming is real and threatening, the political debate that surrounds the science is one of contestation, tension and unwelcomed disruption. Such terms could be applied to the life and work of **Val Plumwood**. Often working as an independent scholar, Plumwood is described as assertive, controversial, provocative and radical in her challenges to established intellectual, political and institutional norms. Central to the challenges she poses are the refutation of dualisms that separated human from non-human or, as Agnes Bolsø puts it, the false division of 'reason, mind and consciousness on one side, and the body, the animal and the pre-human inferiors on the other'. Val Plumwood rejects the portrait of humans as 'disembodied, disembedded and discontinuous' on the basis that it is precisely such positioning that has separated us from our environment and led to the exploitation of the latter. The response, as Agnes notes, is to position humans as part of a differentiated yet interconnected cycle in which organizing recognizes both difference and interdependencies. There are to be no universal solutions or quick organizational fixes. Instead, managers, workers, consumers and policy makers are required to attend to and organize around the particularities of specific contexts and their wider relations.

Underpinning the accounts of Maria Ossowska and of Val Plumwood is a need to challenge how knowledge is constructed and applied if we are to better account for our place in the world. Banu Özkazanç-Pan develops this theme in respect of the transdisciplinary work of **Gayatri C. Spivak**. Chapter 4 describes a writer whose contributions to literature, feminist theories and postcolonial studies have challenged what we think we know about the world and its politics. Developing the concept of the subaltern, Spivak encourages us look in new ways at people(s) we have previously ignored. Her work is important in ethical terms because it challenges our taken-for-granted assumptions about the neutrality of history, including historical methods for accounting for the self and other. It recognizes that, depending on who has the power to write our histories and shape our nation-states, certain 'others' will be ignored, marginalized and suppressed. The argument in this chapter is that this is precisely what is at stake in respect of South East Asia (and the global south and 'Third World' more broadly) when faced with the colonizing power of western thought that renders other forms of knowing and being inferior. Such inferiority arises because of the insistence that the 'other' engage with the West according to the latter's epistemic rules, thus ensuring that the 'other' is always placed at a disadvantage. Banu Özkazanç-Pan argues that Spivak's scholarship offers an alternative. There is an emphasis on the ethicality of breaking the rules that bind people, of focusing on agency and engaging with others rather than adherence to abstract rules. This, in turn, points to the need to think differently if business schools and their alumni are going to be part of rather than separate from the wider world. Overall, Banu draws our attention to the ways in which Gayatri C. Spivak's writing offers a broader and more nuanced understanding of globalization that disrupts the more entrenched concerns of masculinized western thinking and in so doing gives hope to more inclusive futures, while informing subjectivity, ethics and corporate governance.

As we hope is clear by now, one of the joys of organizational studies is its inter-disciplinarity: its willingness to take and learn from other subject areas and fields. Kate Kenny's chapter exemplifies all that is best in this tendency as she introduces us to **Lauren Berlant**. The chapter focuses our attention on what it is like to live and cope with precarity and, relatedly, the burden of cruel optimism. The latter is defined as desiring that prevents us flourishing due to a predilection to pursue dreams that are precarious and even harmful. Specifically, the object(s) of our repeated desires cause us future harm despite our belief that this time it will be different. It is as desire that perhaps explains the UK exit from European Union – a divorce predicated on a recurrent nostalgia for a dream of independence in the face of mounting evidence of, and dissimilation over, the future harms of separatism. Or, as Berlant might have summarized it 'a situation of profound threat that is, at the same time, profoundly confirming' (Berlant, 2011: 2). In organizational terms, we are shown how such cruelty resides in the Fordist myth that hard work and mass consumption will offer up a good life. Putting aside the problems associated with consumption and well-being, Kate Kenny invites us to consider the cruelty of such a promise when placed in front of the many who struggle to survive in a low pay, low trust, making-ends-meet economy. In this way, Lauren Berlant's writing reminds us to look at the bottom of our increasingly unequal societal pyramid rather than at the executives and professions that have for so long preoccupied management studies – no matter how uncomfortable the study of collective precarity may be. Lauren Berlant's methods also make it clear that we can and should utilize literature, film, TV and newspapers to assess societal developments and organization functioning. In short, she challenges us to look again at what we think we know and, as Kate Kenny goes on to discuss, invites us on a different kind of 'ethical noticing'.

In considering the work of **Judith Butler**, the final chapter invites us to look to the future of organizing and managing. Judith Butler is introduced by Nancy Harding as a controversial thinker whose writing spans philosophy, literature, gender, feminism, queer theory and organization studies. More importantly, she is a writer described by Nancy Harding as 'mind-expanding' if complex. Directed at both understanding the constitution of ourselves, while also calling for an active political process aimed at changing the wider world, Butler's work is most closely associated with the notion of performativity. Nancy Harding leads us through the development of the concept as it pertains to the construction of gender binaries; the formation, enactment and sedimentation of identities; and the recursive reinforcement of apparent 'natural' orders. We learn that performativity is not just about words but also the embodied meanings that precede us, are worked through us and flow from us in everyday activities. Nancy Harding draws our attention to the ways in which Butler's work can be used to critique the persistence of established binaries (especially around gender) in management and organization studies, arguing instead for a more nuanced account of organized relations and the power inherent in those embodied, spatial and discursive encounters. The value of Butler's work in ethical and moral terms is implicit in the writing as we consider the injurious nature of words and the casting of certain others as inhuman. This links to what is described as an ethical relation to others predicated on the desire for recognition and an understanding of the ways in which those whose identities disrupt our well-established binaries may be cast-out and unheard.

> The women writers writing about women's philosophy and practice lead us to engage with ethics differently to the ways in which we may do so in mainstream accounts. These writers show us how to embody their new possibilities, the body being a site of responsibility, morality and ethics. This in itself is a way to transgress the very nature of dominant understandings of organization and management especially those that situate ethics at the site of the individual. Instead, we are offered conceptualisations and practices that progress ethics more broadly at the levels of society, community and relationships.

References

Berlant, L.G., 2011. *Cruel optimism*. Durham, NC; London: Duke University Press.

Ford, J., Harding, N. and Learmonth, M., 2008. *Leadership as identity: Constructions and deconstructions*. New York: Springer.

Harding, N. and Palfrey, C., 1997. *The social construction of dementia: Confused professionals?*. Basingstoke: Macmillan.

Harding, N., 2004. *The social construction of management*. London: Routledge.

Harding, N., 2013. *On being at work: The social construction of the employee*. London: Routledge.

2 Forgetting to remember

Maria Ossowska, the giant on whose shoulders I stand

Barbara Czarniawska

Re-discovering the giant

In his book *On the Shoulders of Giants*, Robert Merton (1965/1985) declared that although a received picture of progress in science consists of that idea (attributed to Isaac Newton), in (historical) reality, it is the appointed giants who stand on a pyramid of midgets. But it is a demand of the narrative convention that big discoveries must be made by big heroes; a story about ant-like workers would be dull (Czarniawska, 2009a).

I would like to suggest yet another possibility: that of a midget (myself), who believes to be standing alone, not on the top, but at least in a place with a view, and suddenly discovers that she was, in fact, all the time standing on somebody's shoulders. Was the reason for invisibility that the shoulders belonged to a woman?

This discovery happened in connection with a text I was asked to contribute to a *Festschrift* for Lars Engwall (Sahlin et al., 2009). I had been studying the production of news in news agencies (Czarniawska, 2009c), quite convinced I was alone in this endeavor, when I discovered that Engwall had conducted a similar study 30 years earlier (Engwall, 1981). Thus, sensitized to the possible existence of unknown or forgotten predecessors, I left for my summer vacation in France. I spent some time with my Polish friend who studied psychology together with me at the Warsaw University in the years 1965–1970. In her summerhouse, she had some old books for which she had no room in town. I was looking through them one day, and discovered among them the *Bourgeois Morality* by Polish sociologist Maria Ossowska (1956/1986). As I had recently read Deirdre McCloskey's *The Bourgeois Virtues* (2006), this title attracted my attention and I pulled the dusty volume off the shelf. Ossowska's book, especially the chapter on method, was filled with underlines and annotations. "It was obligatory reading during our second year", my friend said, and I believed her, although I could not recall it.

I decided to re-read the book and discovered that everything I am doing is but an imitation of Ossowska's work. To be more precise, it must be her method chapter that really sunk in. What is more, not only her work has had a great impact on *how* I do research, it has also influenced *what* many of us are studying nowadays. Let me then begin by presenting the author.

Life (1896–1974)

The biography of Maria Ossowska has been presented in several variations (even the alleged day of her birth varies), most likely due to Ossowska's various clashes with authorities that might have led to falsification or loss of documents.[1] Born in January 1896 as Maria Niedźwiecka into an intelligentsia family, as a 14-year-old, she was threatened with disciplinary removal from a school run by nuns – for her heretical opinions. Her dream was to study abroad (there were no Polish universities at the time; Czarniawska and Sevón, 2008), but her parents were against it, and, being a woman, she would have needed their signature to obtain a passport.[2] When the Russians left Warsaw and the new German occupants permitted the opening of the first Polish university in 1915, she enrolled into the Faculty of Philosophy. A year later she had become the Chair of the Philosophical Circle of Warsaw University Students, where she met her future husband.

She defended her doctoral dissertation in 1921. Then she could finally realize her dream; she spent two years at Sorbonne, from where she contacted Bertrand Russell, whose work became of central interest to her. She later visited him in London and maintained a continuous correspondence.

She accepted the post as Assistant Professor at the Philosophy Seminar at Warsaw University in 1923. In 1924 she married Stanisław Ossowski and changed her last name to Ossowska.[3] Until 1929 she taught psychology and pedagogy at the Higher School of Education in Warsaw (observe the fluidity of disciplinary borders at the time).

Bertrand Russell's ontology became the topic of her *habilitation* (the work required for an Associate Professorship), which she defended in 1932.[4] Afterward, Maria and Stanisław spent the years 1933–1935 in London, on a government scholarship. While in London, financed by the Swedish Aid for Polish Culture, she worked on her book, *Podstawy nauki o moralności* (*Foundations of the Science of Morality*), which was finally published in 1947.

During World War II, the Ossowscy organized underground education in Warsaw and helped to hide people in danger of persecution. As early as December 1939, Ossowska had started an underground seminar on the issues of morality, which continued until 1944. In 1940, an underground Warsaw University began its activities, with Ossowska teaching in the Departments of History and Polish Language. Until the summer of 1944 she taught five courses in philosophy, including her own seminar (philosophy was assumed to be a cornerstone of all humanities and social sciences).

After the war, the couple moved to Łódź University, where Ossowska received a personal Chair in Morality Science. She returned to Warsaw University in 1948, taking the Chair of the History and Theory of Morality, although she never became a member of the ruling party (most chairs were held by party members). In 1952 she joined other intellectuals in signing a letter of protest against the growing oppression of the Stalinist regime. As a result, she was forbidden to teach at the university until 1956 when there was a general relaxation of the regime after Khrushchev's famous condemnation of Stalin. It was then that *Bourgeois Morality* was published in Polish, and Ossowska returned to the Sociology Section of the Faculty of Philosophy at Warsaw University. She resigned from her duties as Chair in 1960, but remained a professor there. In the same year, probably on a sabbatical, she gave a series of lectures at Bernard College, Columbia University in New York, lectures that were published in Polish as *Socjologia moralności* (*Sociology of Morality*, 1963).

In 1967 she was invited by the University of Pennsylvania in Philadelphia to give a series of lectures on morality. These lectures, along with the Bernard College lectures, were the basis of her next book, *Social Determinants of Moral Ideas* (1970). In 1972, Ossowska was awarded a first-degree Polish National Award, the highest accolade of the Polish state.

A Polish sociologist and present politician, Jacek Kurczewski, wrote this about her:

> Ossowska was a feminist in the meaning that was given to the word in those times. (…) In prejudices against women she saw one of the fundamental intellectual errors, and herself [sic] concentrated on what was considered the most inappropriate for a learned woman: sex and war.[5]

It has been claimed that in a speech given during the celebration of 50 years of her scientific career in 1969, Ossowska said that throughout her life in science, she did what she wanted, and was even lucky enough to be paid for it.

It can be added that, during her life and afterward, Ossowska was more successful by academic standards than her husband. Nevertheless, a review of the English translation of *Bourgeois Morality* (Szelenyi, 1988) presented this seminal work as though it was an appendix to Stanisław Ossowski's work. Contemporary Polish sociologists, however, euphemistically characterize Ossowski's scientific and political stance as "naive" (Kojder, 2005), and give Maria Ossowska her due, calling her the most erudite, talented and systematic researcher and an independent scholar of unparalleled integrity.

I will now review the areas in which Ossowska's work has influenced mine – whether I was aware of it or not.

The origins of SST

During my time at Warsaw University, studies of science and technology (SST) were unknown to me but have become well known since. Imagine my surprise when I learned that Maria Ossowska and her husband, sociologist Stanislaw Ossowski, are considered by many scholars to be the founders of the field of science studies. In 1935, they published a paper titled "Nauka o nauce" ("The Science of Science"[6]) in the Polish journal *Nauka Polska* (*Polish Science*), which was published in English in a Polish review, *Organon,* in 1936. It was later reprinted in the international journal, *Minerva,* in 1964,[7] and in an edited volume in 1982.

The authors did not claim to have invented anything – on the contrary, they said that interest in science was very old, but it had previously been expressed mostly from an epistemological point of view, focusing on cognitive processes. What was relatively new, they said, was a kind of anthropological interest – science as a part of culture, and science as a social practice:

> It [this new interest] was partly derived from historical research, partly called forth by the development of modern sociology, and partly by practical needs (the question of encouragement and organisation of Science).
>
> (Ossowska and Ossowski, 1935/1964, p. 73)

They continued by suggesting that this new interest could be expressed in at least five different ways, or in five different subfields:

- philosophy of science,
- psychology of science,
- sociology of science,
- organization of science, and
- history of science.

They paid most attention to the sociology of science, locating a similarly minded group of German sociologists (including Karl Mannheim), who dedicated themselves to *Wissenssoziologie* (sociology of knowledge), and found an article by Florian Znaniecki on the same subject preceding the work of the Germans.

The issue arose, however, of whether or not this new science of science deserved a special place as a discipline, or at least a subdiscipline, within the university. I find their answer to that question characteristic of Ossowska's own career and way of thinking:

> From the theoretical point of view this is an insignificant matter. To a large extent it is a matter of convention whether we shall recognize a certain system of problems as a separate branch of learning, or whether we shall subordinate it to a more general science or assign it to several various branches. But as certain practical consequences are involved here, we shall for a moment consider it... (p. 77) A new grouping of problems adds additional importance to the original problems and gives rise to new ones and to new ideas. The new grouping marks out the direction of new investigations, moreover that it may exercise an influence on university studies, the foundation of chairs, periodicals and societies.
>
> (1935/1964, p. 80)

It is clear that the authors were already extremely knowledgeable about the way science works. Curiously enough, the issue of the autonomy – or lack of autonomy – of SST has still not been decided, however, Ossowscy strongly argued for it. Yet there was no doubt as to its growing importance.

As I said before, I was not aware of Ossowska's pioneering contribution to SST until recently. Sometimes the giants are hidden by the clouds in which they reside. But let me move to an influence that undoubtedly did take place in my career: reading the "obligatory lecture" in 1966.

Bourgeois Morality (1956/1986): a brief summary

The book begins with the observation that, at the end of the 19th and beginning of the 20th century, various European countries witnessed a sharp critique of what was called a "bourgeois morality". This critique was as strong in countries with a dominant middle class as it was in countries where the middle class was insignificant. Furthermore, it came from at least three different ideological perspectives: the leftists, the gentry, and the bohemians.

After having briefly summarized those critiques, Ossowska began to search for the epitome of the bourgeois morality expressed in a text or texts. Her choice was Benjamin Franklin, whose model of the human being included *financial reliability*, based on hard work, thrift, orderliness, prudence, and monetary calculation, and a *non-elitist* independence, based on everyday gain. Ossowska showed how these ideas were transformed into the petty bourgeois bible as illustrated by the US sociologists Robert and Helen Lynd in their *Middletown* (1929). Her text also works back in time, situating Franklin's predecessors, and shows that apparently opposite ideologies have a common background. Daniel Defoe's writings on "the complete tradesman" and "the complete gentleman" reveal the process of transformation of the "gentleman" model under the pressure of the bourgeois, who claimed the model as their own. Ossowska also scrutinized Weber's thesis on the origins of capitalism, and, although she was prepared to give Calvinism a key role in the process, pointed out the exceptions to this rule and the impact of other social factors. Under scrutiny was also the Danish sociologist Svend Ranulf's (1938) thesis that envy is the major element of bourgeois morality.

Having analyzed bourgeois morality as a kind of ideology, formulated either by its adherents or (more often) by its critics, Ossowska moved to the issue of moral practices. She addressed three cases: early capitalism (15th century) in Italy, the French Revolution, and the uneasy interaction between the gentry and the bourgeois in 19th-century Poland.

The book ends with two chapters dedicated to methodological reflection: the first addresses the approaches used – by former analysts and Ossowska herself – in the study of bourgeois morality; the second addresses the approach used in the text, especially the usefulness of ideal types as an analytical instrument (my friend's notes were especially visible in these parts of the text as these were apparently important for our exams).

Poaching and trespassing

Whereas, on various occasions, I have made a great deal of fuss about "poaching" (an expression of Michel de Certeau) from disciplines other than my own (Czarniawska, 2008a), Ossowska did not consider the borrowing she did as "poaching", but as normal procedure. The *Bourgeois Morality* moves, without exclamations and caveats, swiftly and expertly between philosophy, economics, history, sociology, and psychology, thereby covering all the disciplines I have poached at one time or another. It does not mean that Ossowska was unaware of disciplinary borders. On the contrary, she made a methodological point of the observation that, blinded by disciplinary borders, sociologists often do not notice how they unreflectively introduce psychological or economic axioms into their reasoning. According to Ossowska, moving across disciplines helps to avoid this kind of unreflective reasoning.

It is possible that the confidence with which Ossowska crossed the disciplinary borders (of whose practical importance she was well aware, as is clear from the previously discussed paper) depended on the fact that she was a philosopher by training, and at that time philosophy was still the queen of all the sciences. But she was also critical of philosophy, as I note later in this text.

Perhaps the most striking trait of the book is that it uses novels as field material. Again, Ossowska presented as quite obvious some of the deepest insights that I have struggled to formulate (Czarniawska, 2009b). It is not the case that novels always contain correct sociological observations; they can tell what does happen in the field or what should take place in a given field. To use Todorov's (1970) terms, one needs to distinguish between the fictional and the fantastic. Thus, to use a contemporary example, the detective novels by Helen Thursten describe (correctly in my view, see Czarniawska, 2011) what happens in Gothenburg's police department, whereas detective novels by Camilla Läckberg describe what should have happened on the West Coast of Sweden if police followed the models of the US soaps. How to tell the difference? Easy – Ossowska would have answered. By comparing them with other texts – other novels and also other texts that formulate the philosophies and ideologies of a given time and place, sometimes by the same author, as was the case with Defoe.

The uses of popular culture

One of my claims (Czarniawska and Rhodes, 2006; Czarniawska and Gustavsson, 2008) is that popular culture – novels, but not only novels – is an important but neglected source of field material to be analyzed by management and organization theories. I encourage my doctoral students to cultivate an interest in it. Claes Ohlsson (2007), for example, studied texts, the aim of which was to convince Swedish people to invest in stock markets. Imagine my surprise when I found in Ossowska's book an analysis of the brochure issued by Polish Saving Bank (PKO) in 1948. A product of the new, socialist regime, it revealed to Ossowska's critical eye strong sediments of the capitalist past ("For the sociologist, it is intriguing to see the detritus of the past continuing by force of inertia into the present", p. 123). The title of the brochure was "Industry and Frugality", alluding (unknowingly?) to the beginning of Benjamin's Franklin's maxim "Be industrious and frugal, and you will be rich". The text of the brochure continued in the same spirit and ended with the (probably unintentional) allusion to a version of Aesop's fable about an ant and a grasshopper by Russian fabulist Ivan Krylov (1769–1844). All summer long, the ant was working and saving, the grasshopper was singing and now wanted a loan; "go and dance then", answered the ant. The Polish Saving Bank said almost the same thing, and in verse form. Having compared the two texts, Ossowska hastened to assure readers that:

> I am not concerned with taking the author of this pamphlet to task. After all, it is hardly surprising that any attempt to boost the virtue of thriftiness should have to tread well-worn paths, given the amount of propaganda devoted to this theme in bourgeois literature; though the climate of this propaganda should perhaps be recognized as alien in the new conditions, and in conflict (as in the fable of the ant and the cricket) with the ideals of socialism. Nor it is my purpose to develop an anatomy of thrift which would be in keeping with the new social structure and with the guidelines of life in a socialist society.
>
> (1986, p. 125)

Not only did she refuse to issue a prescription (I return to her reluctance to be normative), she also poked fun at the authorities in a very serious text published under serious circumstances.

Accounting and gender

Had I rediscovered Ossowska's book earlier, it would have helped me to write my paper on "Accounting and Gender across Times and Places" (Czarniawska, 2008b), in which I tried to explain why accounting, historically and now, has been a women's occupation in Poland. My thesis was that accounting was one of the most attractive jobs offered to noblewomen from impoverished families (from which came the majority of noblewomen at the turn of the 19th century). Trade was considered beyond their dignity, whereas teaching (at the elementary level), although it was believed that it did not require any talents but some education, did not suit all temperaments. I have argued for my thesis with the aid of Polish novels from that period but was unaware of a novel called *The Princess* by Zofia Urbanowska, which would have further strengthened my argument.

The novel's central character is namely a daughter of a bankrupt nobleman who goes to Warsaw to earn her living and is given housing and work by a bourgeois family (thus Ossowska's interest in the novel). The mother of the family tells the young woman: "Accounts are like a mirror – in them I see my understanding of life, my mistakes, sometimes also my good side. The account book is our mentor, our historian, our conscience" (quoted after Ossowska, 1986, p. 99). And the son of the family completes the instruction: "I suggest you learn how to keep accounts as quickly as possible. Accounting is the basis of all social order..." (ibid). Thus, while many young women in other countries sought jobs as teachers, many Polish women chose the career of a bookkeeper.

My only consolation in having missed such an important piece of evidence is that Ossowska admits to being alerted to that work by Jan Kott (a famous literary critic, who moved to the United States in 1966 and became a renowned Shakespeare critic). On the shoulders, at the feet, or arm in arm, research is a collective endeavor, performed by what Peirce called a community on inquiry (see e.g. Swedberg, 2014, p. 28).

At this point, I would also underline Ossowska's brand of feminism, which has been my ideal, but of which I still fall short. Never using the word, and never emphasizing her contribution, she constantly quoted women authors and analyzed the role of women in various editions of bourgeois morality.

With eye close to the ground

As I have mentioned, Ossowska distanced herself from traditional philosophical pursuits. Her interest was in the everyday minutiae of great, sweeping ideologies, and she was keenly aware of the unorthodoxy of her analytical method:

> The researcher accustomed to working on purely philosophical themes in which conceptual analysis has a crucial role to play if the product is to be a genuine contribution to philosophy, is bound to feel daunted when confronted with the limitless sea of facts which go to form the history of human culture. As one burrows one's way into philosophical theories and concepts one feels – perhaps mistakenly – that one is in control of the material, and that it can be interpreted with some degree of precision. Not so here: the deeper one penetrates into the subject, the more one is convinced that some facts are escaping, eluding one's grasp; or

that the very next source to be explored will force revaluation of one's whole carefully constructed picture of reality. We can never have the satisfaction of knowing that the ground has been covered, the material exhausted.

(1986: viii)

Observe the subtlety of this statement: she did not criticize the methods of philosophy, and yet the text makes it obvious that they are inadequate for the purpose of studying human culture. The methods that are available – she describes the operation of abduction[8] here, briefly, correctly, and unpretentiously – seem to be full of weaknesses, and yet somehow these weaknesses seem to be their strength. One wishes that doctoral students could learn this way of presenting their methodology – without attacking the enemy and without defending themselves from criticisms not yet uttered.

Reflexivity absorbed

Another trait of Ossowska's texts that I admire lies in her skillful use of reflexivity. I call it "reflexivity absorbed", because the issue as such never enters her pages. She was also not prone to tell the readers details of her life, but revealed exactly what was needed, when it was needed, and in the amount needed:

3. A note on the growth of this study
It was during the German occupation of Poland that I begun to study the problem of bourgeois morality; and my intention was to demonstrate the class character of morality to those who still believed it to be homogenous and above class. As my starting point I took Benjamin Franklin, and the first edition[9] of the present work opened with my discussion of this writer. In the course of further study, however, it became clear that this particular choice was prompted by a subconscious conviction that I already knew what bourgeois morality was. Faced with a wide range of moralists of bourgeois provenance, why had I chosen Franklin to illustrate bourgeois morality? It could only be because in my mind's eye he already figured as an embodiment of it. Which in turn suggested that, if Franklin could figure as its paradigm, a preconceived notion of bourgeois morality was already present in my mind. (...)[9]

So how did I acquire my preconceived idea of bourgeois morality? Today I do not doubt that what played a large part here was the criticism leveled at the unhappy bourgeois from many quarters in several countries in the second half of the 19th century and the first quarter of the 20th (1986, p. 14).

She thus examined herself step by step, and what she discovered only reconfirmed her choice of material. It is exactly the eulogies, apologies, and criticisms of the bourgeois morality that she analyzed in her work.

Against normativity

In a tribute to Maria Ossowska's integrity and talent, Andrzej Kojder (2005) wrote that Ossowska programmatically avoided normative postulates in her work. This trait was highly original for two reasons. The first was that socialist writers, whether scientists or not, were supposed to come up with prescriptions and instructions for the people of the new socialist republic. The second was that, irrespective of the political regime, issuing prescriptions – theoretical or methodological – is the common way of establishing schools of thought and attracting followers. The only exception was a pamphlet with the title *The Model of the Citizen in the Democratic System*,[10] and its existence can be explained by the fact that it was written in 1946, before the new regime enforced strict censorship. The very use of the adjective "democratic" rather than "socialist" indicates the recklessness of such an endeavor. What is more, this ideal democratic citizen was supposed to have a sense of beauty and a sense of humor – the latter serving as the ultimate protection against the temptations of totalitarianism.

By the time of *Bourgeois Morality*, Maria Ossowska was clear about where she stood: closely approaching reality with an acknowledgment of plurality and no moral judgments. Her task was to study moralities, not to moralize. The English version of the book ends with the following sentences:

> Whether the attempt made in this book to establish such general truths [concerning classic types of bourgeois moral thought] has been successful or not, the author hopes that the reader is now in a better position to judge what actually *does* take place in the field where it has been customary to consider only what *ought* to take place. By the same token, a belief in "morality" as a constant may well yield to the realisation that many variants of morality may coexist – even in one and the same society.
>
> (1986, p. 368)

The question of style

Last but not least, I was surprised by Ossowska's style. By now I am used to the fact that when reviewers call something "essayistic", it means a harsh critique, not a compliment. But I still think highly of the essayistic style, and this is how she wrote. The certainty of the tone of natural sciences – or philosophy – does not fit the students of human culture, who "can never have the satisfaction of knowing that the ground has been covered, the material exhausted". I also recall that in the 1970s, when I was a young researcher, Ossowska came to be considered "not scientific enough". As McCloskey (1985) so convincingly demonstrated, it was in the 1970s when "writing badly" became "writing well" in economics (and I would claim, in most social sciences) – when the rhetoric of scientism came to rule. Ossowska was free from that rule, which does not mean that she wrote like a journalist or a management consultant, but that she wrote well – I would say, like a literary critic, but perhaps here I am retrojecting my own values onto my idol.

Forgetting to remember

If it had not been for the accidental finding of the book on my friend's shelf, I would not have even remembered it. I have three possible explanations of both my imitation and my lack of awareness – explanations that can actually be complementary rather than competing.

The first is simple forgetting. It does not have to be treated as a vice, if one accepts Michel Oakeshott's (1959/1991) idea that science does not accumulate – that it is a conversation that continues for centuries. It may temporarily improve in style or in politeness, or equally temporarily worsen in those respects, and it includes more and more participants. But conversation it is. In such conversations, it is quite possible that certain topics recur either because the participants have been exchanged and the new group does not remember previous conversation topics or because those who participated in the previous one forgot it, internalizing its precepts as their own (as I did).

The second explanation is somewhat paradoxical, as the omission is explained by similarity. Gilbert (1977) proved that authors are least prone to reference properly those authors whose work is the closest to their own. It is the perception of difference that prompts referencing.

The third explanation is a cyclical topicality of certain issues. After all, Deirdre McCloskey's *The Bourgeois Virtues* can be seen as a new version of Ossowska's *Bourgeois Morality*, the former written without any knowledge of the latter, as the English version of Ossowska's book is little known and out of print. Bruno Latour (2002), to quote another example, recently appointed Gabriel Tarde as his scientific ancestor, although he has read him only now.

In any case, the image of a pyramid of giants, interspersed with midgets, is not convincing. Maybe, in the conversation of science, some say more and some listen more. Then the listeners go home and try to repeat the most attractive arguments for the use of the wider circle.

My messages to the wider circle based on what I have learned from Ossowska would be two: transdisciplinarity and style. Like she, I believe that the vocation of social sciences is to study social phenomena, and that we can be useful without being normative. Social phenomena do not follow the division into traditional disciplines, and in order to describe, explain and interpret such phenomena (choose your favorite verb) one can get help from whichever field that is of help. Perhaps Ossowska's and my predilection for literature and popular culture does not have to be followed by all (luckily, there are quite few who do it), but all social sciences and humanities can offer useful insights (and so do natural sciences, of course).

As to style, Michael Billig (2013) did a good job ridiculing the pretentious non-style of academic publications, whereas I took up positive models in our field (Czarniawska, 2003). Still, I can't resist pointing out that reading good novels[11] – and great predecessors – helps to write well.

Recommended reading

Original text by Maria Ossowska

Ossowska, Maria (1986) *Bourgeois morality (1986)*. London: Routledge and Kegan Paul.

Key academic text

Szelenyi, Ivan (1988) Maria Ossowska: Bourgeois morality. *European Sociological Review*, 4(3): 284–285.

Accessible resource

Maria Ossowska: Contexts and Inspirations Conference on the 40th Anniversary of her Death University of Warsaw, 24–25 October 2014. http:// polish-sociological-review.eu/wp-content/uploads/2015/02/PSR188-08.pdf

Notes

1 I decided to rely primarily on a recent work by Masarczyk (2008).
2 Or her husband, had she been married.
3 The Polish surnames in an adjective form change with gender: Maria Ossowska, Stanisław Ossowski, the married couple Ossowscy.
4 Another date has been quoted as 1925, which seems unlikely to me.
5 (http://www.forumakad.pl/archiwum/2005/03/26-gwiazy_i_meteory.htm, accessed 2/3/2010, translation BC). Sex was obviously one of the important topics in the discussion about bourgeois morality, while war came across in another of her topics: chivalrous ethos.
6 It needs to be added that in Polish "science" does not have the Anglo-Saxon association with natural sciences.
7 The editor's introduction again concentrated on the importance of Stanisław Ossowski's thoughts, although Maria was the first author; but it could have been an expression of respect due to the fact that Stanisław had recently died.
8 Abduction is a method of logical inference introduced by the U.S. pragmatist Charles Sanders Peirce, which comes prior to induction and deduction, and which in colloquial language is called "a hunch". For a good description of abduction see Eco and Sebeok (1988).
9 The English translator made a mistake here: in the Polish text it says "in the first drafts".
10 It was reprinted in 1992 as *The Paragon of a Democrat: Virtues and Values*.
11 Though it is not quite certain whether or not good novels lead to a better management... (Czarniawska-Joerges and Guilled de Monthoux, 1994).

References

Billig, Michael (2013) *Learn to write badly: How to succeed in the social sciences*. Cambridge, UK: Cambridge University Press.

Czarniawska, Barbara (1997) *Narrating the organization. The drama of institutional identity*. Chicago, IL: University of Chicago Press.

Czarniawska, Barbara (2003) The styles and the stylists of organization theory. In Tsoukas, Haridimos and Knudsen, Christian (eds.) *The Oxford handbook of organization theory*. Oxford: Oxford University Press, 237–261.

Czarniawska, Barbara (2008a) *A theory of organizing*. Cheltenham: Edward Elgar.

Czarniawska, Barbara (2008b) Accounting and gender across times and places: An excursion into fiction. *Accounting, Organizations and Society*, 33(1): 33–47.

Czarniawska, Barbara (2009a) Emerging institutions: Pyramids or anthills? *Organization Studies*, 30(4): 422–441.

Czarniawska, Barbara (2009b) Distant readings: An anthropology of organizations through novels. *Journal of Organizational Change Management*, 22(4): 357–372.

Czarniawska, Barbara (2009c) My forgotten predecessors. In Sahlin, Kerstin, Wedlin, Linda, and Grafström, Maria (eds.) *Exploring the worlds of Mercury and Minerwa*. Uppsala: Acta Universitatis Upsaliensis, 101–112.

Czarniawska, Barbara (2011) How to study gender inequality in organizations? In Jeanes, Emma L., Knights, David, and Martin, Patricia (eds.) *Handbook of gender, work and organization*. Chichester: Wiley-Blackwell, 81–108.

Czarniawska, Barbara, and Gustavsson, Eva (2008) A (d)evolution of the cyberwoman? *Organization*, 15(5): 665–683.

Czarniawska, Barbara, and Rhodes, Carl (2006) Strong plots: Popular culture in management practice and theory. In Gagliardi, Pasquale and Czarniawska, Barbara (eds.) *Management education and humanities*. Cheltenham: Edward Elgar, 195–218.

Czarniawska, Barbara, and Sevón, Guje (2008) The thin end of the wedge: Foreign women professors as double strangers in academia. *Gender, Work and Organization*, 15(3): 235–287.

Czarniawska-Joerges, Barbara, and Guillet de Monthoux, Pierre (eds.) (1994) *Good novels, better management*. Reading, MA: Harwood.

Eco, Umberto, and Sebeok, Thomas (eds.) (1988) *The sign of the three: Dupin, Holmes, Peirce*. Bloomington, IN: Indiana University Press.

Engwall, Lars (1981) *Newspapers as organizations*. Aldershot: Gower.

Gilbert, Nigel G. (1977) Referencing as persuasion. *Social Studies of Science*, 7: 113–122.

Kojder, Andrzej (2005) Maria Ossowska – uczona integralna. *Etyka*, 38: 87–90.

Latour, Bruno (2002) Gabriel Tarde and the end of the social. In Joyce, Patrick (ed.) *The social in question. New bearings in the history and the social sciences*. London: Routledge, 117–132.

Lynd, Robert, and Lynd, Helen (1929) *Middletown, a study of American culture*. New York: Harcourt, Brace & Co.

Masarczyk, Rafal (2008) *Granice relatywizmu w filozofii moralnosci Marii Osowskiej*. Kraków: Wydawnictwo Salwator.

McCloskey, D.N. (1985) *The rhetoric of economics*. Madison, WI: The University of Wisconsin Press.

McCloskey, D.N. (2006) *The bourgeois virtues*. Chicago, IL: University of Chicago Press.

Merton, Robert K. (1965/1985) *On the shoulders of giants. A Shandean postscript*. New York: Harcourt & Jovanovich.

Oakeshott, Michael (1959/1991) The voice of poetry in the conversation of mankind. In *Rationalism in politics and other essays*. Indianapolis, IN: Liberty Press, 488–541.

Ohlsson, Claes (2007) *Folkets fonder? En textvetenskaplig studie av det svenska pensionssparandets domesticering*. Gothenburg: University of Gothenburg Press.

Ossowska, Maria (1956) *Moralność mieszczańska*. Warszawa: PWN. English version: *Bourgeois morality* (1986) London: Routledge and Kegan Paul.

Ossowska, Maria (1970) *Social determinants of moral ideas*. Philadelphia, PA: University of Pennsylvania Press.

Ossowska, Maria and Ossowski, Stanisław (1935) Nauka o nauce. *Nauka Polska*, XX (3). In English: The science of science, *Minerva*, 1964, III (1): 72–82. Reprinted in: Walentynowicz, Bohdan (ed.), 1982, *Polish contributions to the science of science*. Berlin: Springer, 82–95.

Ranulf, Svend (1938) *Moral indignation and middle class psychology: A sociological study*. New York: Schicken Books.

Sahlin, Kerstin, Wedlin, Linda, and Grafström, Maria (eds.) (2009) *Exploring the worlds of Mercury and Minerwa*. Uppsala: Acta Universitatis Upsaliensis.

Swedberg, Richard (2014) From theory to theorizing. In Swedberg, Richard (ed.) *Theorizing in social science: The context of discovery*. Stanford, CA: Stanford University Press, 1–28.

Szelenyi, Ivan (1988) Maria Ossowska: Bourgeois morality. *European Sociological Review*, 4(3): 284–285.

Todorov, Tzvetan (1970/1975) *The fantastic. A structural approach to a literary genre*. Ithaca, NY: Cornell University Press.

3 Val Plumwood

Organizing for the future

Agnes Bolsø

If you are looking for alternative ideas about how humans could organize themselves in times of global warming, the Australian philosopher Val Plumwood (1939–2008) has much to offer. She engages with two of the most prolific streams of ideas since the 1970s: feminism and environmentalism. Plumwood's highly original thinking draws on the basic ecofeminist idea that women and nature are both seen as inferior in a long tradition of Western philosophy and religion, and that this must come to an end. My aim in writing this chapter is to demonstrate her relevance while thinking about organizations in times such as ours and also to provide a sense of her life as interwoven with her ideas.

Stories we live by

To grant Val Plumwood the irrefutable place within contemporary Organization Studies that she deserves, one first has to acknowledge the significance of stories and narratives in the lives of *Homo sapiens*. In his bold sweep through the history of humankind in his international bestseller, one of Yuval Noah Harari's more convincing points is how fiction and myth-creating are characteristic of us. *Homo sapiens* are capable of speaking 'about things that don't really exist' (Harari 2015: 27). We can imagine things and – most importantly – we can do so collectively. We can create large social units based on myths (e.g. national, religious or economic), and this makes us unrivalled in terms of cooperation. This is, of course, a widespread insight within Organization Studies (OS) already. The conceptualizations, images, narratives and language that we use have a bearing on how we actually organize ourselves (Morgan 2006). Our use of imagery plays a role in an 'interactive, emergent process through which we are constantly engaging in shaping science, knowledge creation and the everyday world' (Morgan 2016: 1040). Shifting imaginaries potentially have a huge influence on the development of both organizations and society. In her analysis of the Global Financial Crisis of 2007–2010, Barbara Czarniawska demonstrates the need for 'new plots' in finance (2012). *In the case of Plumwood, we are talking about a new image of the relationship between humans and other forms of life on earth.* We have to change the way in which we organize our economy and, in particular, how we use natural resources and other non-human organisms for our livelihood. This has *everything* to do with how we imagine ourselves and others. In our immediate future, this shift will both rely on *and* impact upon practitioners in organizations, and OS must try to keep up.

It is not for me to suggest these new imageries for how *Homo sapiens* must organize to be ecologically sustainable. I aim, however, to offer significant elements by selecting the ideas from Plumwood that I have found to be most pertinent in the context of organizations. The chapter revolves around topics such as food, death and our relationship with nature; topics that are crucial for all societies at all times. However, *we* must think anew and stop living by the stories that have got the planet into so much trouble. We must reorganize on every level, not least our minds, and, as Plumwood argues, we must find ways around the *dualist* way of conceptualizing matters of the world in Western thought.

The general critique of dualism

Val Plumwood systematically and historically criticizes dualisms in Western traditions of thought, which aligns her with the 1980s and 1990s wave of poststructuralist work. Her critique of dualisms is not just a few introductory lines, a paragraph or two before she moves on to what is really her errand. No, this *is* her errand. Dualism is the process by which contrasting concepts (for example, masculine and feminine gender identities) are formed by domination and subordination and constructed as oppositional and exclusive. She demonstrates the profound structure of insurmountable differences in Western thought between, for instance, culture/nature; reason/nature; male/female; mind/body; master/slave; reason/matter; rationality/animality; reason/emotion; mind, spirit/nature; freedom/necessity; universal/particular; human/nature; human/non-human; civilized/primitive; production/reproduction; public/private; subject/object; self/other (1993: 43). Nature as the excluded and devalued contrast to reason includes, she says, 'the emotions, the body, the passion, animality, the primitive and uncivilized, the non-human world, matter, physicality and sense experience, as well as the sphere of irrationality, of faith and madness' (1993: 20). We need to think of nature as an agent, and we need to think of the presence of nature not an absence of people, but nature as a partner. This implies that she is insisting on a radical reorganizing of our minds, our ways of thinking and imagining. And, first, mind is not to be thought of as separate from the body. Your mind is embedded in your material reality and in your body, and the distinction cannot be thought of as a separation between completely different substances. This also implies that Val Plumwood must be read in parallel with the life she lived.

Walking the talk

Born in relative poverty on the outskirts of Sydney just before World War II, roaming the bush as a child, partly home-schooled, there was little sign that she would become an influential albeit institutionally marginalized philosopher – she, a girl, a woman long before a general acknowledgement of women's worth in academia. It was also way too early for the Pill, not to mention abortion rights, which meant that pregnancy was destiny for many women in Australia, as it was in other parts of the world at that time. The following experiences seem to have characterized her early life: a first-hand knowledge of nature, experiential learning outside in the world and not in a scholarly institution, getting pregnant and becoming a mother at a young age, having the urge to learn and a sense of not being properly acknowledged for her ideas. These experiences form the perfect foundation for a romanticization of Plumwood: an outsider who became an intellectual woman against all the odds. *That* story could also be told, perhaps, but it would be a choice not so easy to defend. She was far too controversial, quarrelsome and provocative to be reduced to someone who victoriously 'made it'. Also, her strained relationship with institutions made it difficult for her to be or feel successful, or indeed be seen as one marked by success. Val's close friend, the Australian author Jackie French, puts it like this: 'Val was far too vivid to be recreated as an eco saint, a sort of Mother Theresa on her mountain. She enjoyed being who she was enormously. She would hate to be diminished into a respectable stereotype now' (French 2008: 5).

Profound radical thinking is often, if not always, born out of lives lived in dissonance with their surroundings, and this was definitely the case here. Plumwood had to *live* her ideas – she wanted to learn from nature and needed her ideas to be developed in reciprocity through a particular way of life. Hers was an intellectual endeavour at odds with conventional academic practices. This Routledge book series is about neglected academic women, but Plumwood resisted and shunned institutionalized academia throughout her life. It was in some sense mutual neglect and rejection and, as far as I can tell, it was probably a frustrating relation for both parties.

When I agreed to write about Val Plumwood, I read the biography of her and her long-term partner, husband and colleague, philosopher Richard Sylvan by Dominic Hyde and (2014). Even before, I had been impressed and inspired by Plumwood's lucid and powerful thinking, but the well-informed and critical biography, so carefully and lovingly written by Hyde, led me to wonder about the lives of this couple. Within what context did Val Plumwood develop her thoughts? How did life events influence her ways of thinking and vice versa?

Before I turn to these and other questions, I would like to reflect on my feeling of connectedness to Val Plumwood. It is a long way from Val's all-year-around sunny Australia to my Norway, with its long harsh winters; between Val the philosopher and me the sociologist; between Val's stubborn protest against any restraints put on her own thinking by institutional power and me going along with it, and rather dutifully albeit on a bumpy road, becoming a full professor, embodying the university institution myself. I have come to think that the connection goes via nature and landscapes. We both grew up in rural areas, getting a sense of our bodies and ourselves as distinctively implied in our natural surroundings – both becoming radicals, she in the late 1960s and I in the early 1970s, this feeling of earthiness became part of our radicalism. She, the philosopher outside a university, lived in the wilderness and developed a quite impressive philosophy about humans and nature. I, then still a young Marxist sociologist, broke off my university studies in the city to move back to the countryside and make a living from agricultural work on non-industrial and small-scale farms, seeing myself as part of the agricultural working class, contributing to a sustainable future. Feminism always had a central place in her thinking, as it had in my sense of politics.

However, she was a frontrunner in forms of poststructural and critical thinking that were unfamiliar to me as a young academic, and I guess a bit foreign to most social scientists trained in more structuralist forms of theory at that time. When I worked on environmental issues in the 1970s and 1980s, I would understand our problems in the light of capitalist and imperialist overuse and exploitation. Plumwood's approach makes it clear how deeply involved we all are in the exploitation of other humans, non-humans and natural resources, and that there is more at stake than reorganizing the economy. We are in dire need of new narratives about communication between all the different inhabitants of the earth.

More than ever, we need people working in and with organizations to be interested in the relationship between organizations, societies and politics, as well as organizations per se – organizing for the future needs the philosophers, the sociologists, the economists, the administration and management scholars, the art people, the activists and more. In short, we need cross- and interdisciplinary cooperation of magnitude, some would even say *trans*disciplinary work – creative critical thinking and imagining beyond disciplines (Lykke 2010; Haraway 2016).

Field trip

Dominic Hyde's joint biography did more than just stimulate my curiosity. Inspired by this book, I travelled from Norway to Australia for a one-month stay in February 2017. There I did essential reading, communicated with people who had known Val and also wrote the first draft of this chapter. The main event, however, was my visit to Plumwood Mountain and the stone house Val built together with her husband Richard during the second half of the 1970s. Generously hosted by Anne Edwards, the caretaker of the house, I was able to get a sense of the place where Val Plumwood worked and lived during her academically most productive years. In the middle of a damp and misty rainforest, the humble octagonal house stood erect, invisible until you came up close. The rough stone walls had no insulation, and I was shown the holes now inhabited by Australia's most poisonous spiders. Anne lived there and checked her bed for spiders every night. She had yet to find one, though. Very poisonous snakes also lived in the vicinity, but Anne knew exactly where they preferred to linger and would avoid such places. 'I leave them alone, just like they avoid me', Anne said. She guided me to places where Val used to bush walk, where she could sense the forest and its inhabitants and where she would develop her philosophy. I saw (and touched!) the outdoor table and chair where she would often sit and write. How she was able to concentrate is beyond me, because the leeches were everywhere, soundlessly inching their way up our boots. The boots had to be checked every ten minutes and still, under my belt buckle on the train back to Sydney, I discovered that two suckers had made a happy meal of my blood.

The visit added meaning to my own reading. I would read and imagine Plumwood Mountain, where under Anne Edwards' tutoring I had learned that humans and non-humans were both spatially entitled and could live in mutual respect and recognition. I was able to achieve a better understanding of the texts than before. Val is buried on Plumwood Mountain and people who loved her have made a beautiful memorial site, as best they could in accordance with Plumwood's ideas about life and death (Salmon 2008). She was critical of ideas concerning death offered up by the monotheistic religions, and of burial ceremonies and cemeteries. She definitely did not want to be buried in a solid wooden box six feet under in a conventional graveyard, barely accessible to other creatures! Her own burial ceremony on Plumwood Mountain reflects her philosophy of the human body as related to the bodies of other species and to other forms of materiality.

Being part of the food chain

Plumwood's violent encounter with a big Australian saltwater crocodile in 1985 had a strong impact on her thinking; the incident made her acutely aware of being prey, possible sustenance, meat, for another creature. It took more than a decade before she wrote about it, and only then we were to learn in detail about her canoe trip, the sudden attack, the three death rolls and the struggle to survive, which she achieved thanks to the fierce fight she put up and her extensive bush experience (Plumwood 1996). It was important for her to frame the attack within ecological and philosophical frameworks. One needs to tell one's own story and not let it be 'taken over by others and given an alien meaning', not allow it to be stereotyped and sensationalized by the mass media (Plumwood 1999: 86). It was, for instance, important for her to try to prevent the 'massive crocodile slaughter' that might have followed a dramatic crocodile attack such as she experienced (ibid.: 85). The philosophical points she would draw from the experience were further developed and published posthumously in a collection of essays edited by Lorraine Shannon, titled *The Eye of the Crocodile* (Plumwood 2012).

Plumwood had long been aware in some abstract way that humans were animals that sometimes could be eaten by other animals, but then again, she says, 'in some important way, I did *not* know it, absolutely rejected it' (2012: 10). It is with breathtaking intensity that she describes the moment of truth, when a powerful creature ignores her special status as a human being and actually tries to eat her:

> In the vivid intensity of those last moments, when great, toothed jaws descend upon you, it can HIT YOU LIKE A THUNDERCLAP that you were completely wrong about it all – not only about what your own personal life meant, but about what life and death themselves actually mean.
>
> (2012: 11)

She had already been a critic of anthropocentrism for many years when the attack happened; so how was it, she asks, that it seemed so wrong that the crocodile should eat her? Why was she so shocked? What kind of wrong and what kind of shock was it? She proceeds to give some answers that demonstrate how deeply ingrained the thought is in Western culture that humans are set apart from other animals and the rest of nature, 'made unlike them, in the image of God' (2012: 14). Despite Darwin, she argues, we have still only superficially, and mainly on an intellectual level, acknowledged that humans are indeed an animal and are part of the natural order, or rather, natural chaos.[1] We are not only spectators at the feast where animals eat each other, but 'we are the feast' (ibid.: 15), included as embodied, flesh as food, in kinship with others. Plumwood's critique of the dualism between reason, mind and consciousness on one side, and the body, the animal and the pre-human inferior on the other, is well known from her earlier writing. The same goes for her claim that this divide has enabled the exploitation of nature and made us responsible for the ecological crisis. In this posthumous collection of essays, however, she clarifies the double-sided character of the human–nature dualism and the challenge that we are facing. As long as the essential feature of being human is perceived as 'disembodied, disembedded and discontinuous' (ibid.: 16) and that of nature and animals as mindless bodies 'excluded from the realms of ethics and culture' (ibid.: 16), we will have to resituate both humans and nature. The task before us is to integrate and situate human life in ecological terms and non-human life in ethical terms.

The Eye of the Crocodile is the book's title, but it also represents a perspective within the book – it is 'the view of an old eye, an appraising and critical eye that potentially judges the quality of human life and finds it wanting' (ibid.: 16). Such a perspective can help us to see ourselves in a 'more ecologically democratic position' (ibid.: 17). This is not to suggest that Plumwood will allow people to be food for crocodiles, or that she is an ontological vegetarian.[2] She is aiming for a more democratic set of relationships between humans, animals and nature – we must understand that we are each 'made for the other' (ibid.: 18). In order to build new relationships, she insists that we rethink how we understand what it is to be human, what food is and, not least, what *death* is.

Death

The denial that we are food for others is reflected in our burial practices: the strong and heavy coffin that in principle should prevent animals from coming in and feasting on us, the six feet under to avoid soil fauna, the slab on top to prevent us from being dug up – we want to remain apart even in death. Even if our soul, conventionally seen as salvageable, has now departed for a disembodied non-earthly existence, we should still not become food for others; we can eat others, but not be eaten; we can take, but not give. Plumwood's proposal is that 'the food/death imaginary with which we have lost touch is a key to re-imagining ourselves ecologically, as members of a larger community of radical equality, mutual nurturance and support' (ibid.: 19). Hierarchical and exceptionalist cultural frameworks must be displaced and we must look for 'continuity, meaning and hope' in a larger context, the context of an 'earth community' (ibid.: 19). This might sound airy-fairy and quite similar to the holism against which she absolutely positions herself, a holism that implies a cosmic oneness with the universe. Extreme holism is in Plumwood's reasoning not sufficiently aware of either the differences between organisms or the continuities between them. Plumwood actively relates to notions of difference, be it those between humans and non-humans, or those between people. Having looked a crocodile in the eye is a powerful remedy against holism, one might suspect. A philosophy of material and social differences runs through her writing, adding to the political applicability of her ideas.

A compelling critique of the Western idea of the essential self as a spiritual one, disembodied and potentially eternal, is of particular relevance. Simultaneously, it is also a critique of 'the reductive and materialist concept of death as a complete ending', the story of the material embodied self as totally over. The first alienates us from the earth. The cost of the second is the 'loss of meaning and narrative continuity for the self' (Plumwood 2012: 92). Plumwood elaborates upon her double critique. She suggests alternatives, and here she is inspired by indigenous animist concepts of self and death:

> By understanding life as circulation, as a gift from a community of ancestors, we can see death as recycling, a flowing on into an ecological and ancestral community of origins.
>
> (ibid.: 92)

Here we find neither the hope for eternity by projecting human essence onto spirit, nor the abrupt ending of the self-narrative marked by the dead body; here there is a continuity of life narration through circulation, through becoming food for others. We are desperately in need of such alternative understandings, she says. People believe less and less in 'post-earth transcendence' (ibid.: 94) and modernity has not replaced the idea of a spiritual afterlife with anything that is meaningful or comforting. Reductive materialism, Plumwood argues, 'is marked especially by the Finality Thesis, the claim that death is the final *end of the story*. It is this loss of story, the narrative of no narratives, that is expressed in the massive mute modernist headstones' (ibid.: 95). But, of course, the body does not just end. It decays and decomposes, losing its prior form, is incorporated into new forms and shared. The tone is actually rather joyful when she writes about this: 'Lots of linking, after-life narratives here!' (ibid.: 95). As one would expect from a philosopher with an interest in the material, practical and organizational, Plumwood does not only *write* critically about the contemporary administration of dead bodies. She also took part in what she labels 'the cemetery wars', arguing for ecological burial practices (Plumwood 2007).

Plumwood argues that the 'heavenist identification of self with spirit' continues in a scientific, modern and reductionist split between spirit and matter. That there should be no continuity of life after a human being loses consciousness is an acceptance of the dualist Cartesian proposition that our essential element is just that. Losing conscious-ness would signify the loss of self and this is simply wrong because the story goes on, says Plumwood, but it is 'no longer mainly a story about human subjects' (2012: 95). In her 'animist materialism', the afterlife is a 'positive, ecological presence, positive traces in the lives of other species' (ibid.: 95). Some of her ideas about death are reflected in inno-vations in the management of dead human bodies, for instance by the American undertaker Caitlin Doughty (2015, 2017). Human death is, for obvious reasons, a huge industry and one should not be surprised that ecological alternatives constitute a growing market.

Plumwood's ideas about death are embedded in a fluid and yet embodied concept of self – a self that is continuous *and* particular. She emphasizes the distinctions between different species and also the particularities of each human being's attachments and relations.

Self and others

Plumwood found that, in their thinking, influential contemporary ecological and environmental philosophers erased the distinction between the human and the non-human. In their attempt to place humankind in nature, Plumwood traces a continuity within West-ern philosophy of positioning women and non-whites as 'closer to the animal' and 'lacking the full measure of rationality or culture' (Plumwood 1993: 4).[3] With reference to the work of another ecological feminist, Karen Warren, Plumwood criticizes environmental ethics for 'moral extensionism' (ibid.: 159) in which human moral capacity is expanded to also include non-humans. Through this extension, the human subject remains an unmodified Cartesian rational and self-sufficient being. The lack of relationality in the understanding of the human subject as an agent results in a denial of class, gender and nature (Plumwood 1993: 153). This implies that one fights the separation between humans and nature by idealizing their potential for a harmonious coexistence. This idealization excludes specific aspects of both human and non-human others and produces a 'colonizing self' that interacts with others 'only in the image of its own desires or needs, which it imposes upon them' (Plumwood 1993: 158). This problem is intensified by various visions of a society in ecological balance, and ideas of harmonious coexistence between humans and non-humans.

There are boundaries between self and nature, she says, and humans must not think of their selves as encompassing 'the other', nor reject the particularities and relational character of the self (Plumwood 1991, 1993). We cannot establish harmony, not in nature, not in society, not in any relation, states Plumwood. Her idea of self is a relational self, a self in relation to others, which does not, however, imply that it is merged, indistinguishable or lacking in contour. On the contrary, our selves are simultaneously distinct and continuous. She locates distinctions in class, gender and race that must be considered in evaluating green politics for organizations. People are also positioned differently from one another in terms of places that support us and to which we might feel bodily and emotionally connected. Our politics, organizational politics included, must always take this into account.

Organizing communities

We must analyze, and live, the particularities. Implicitly, this is a critique of modelling organizations and institutions according to a universal idea about the optimal. Conceptions of the human, the self and nature connect, and we will have to address this with an eye for the particular. It is to particular places, forests and animals that one is strongly related or attached, and we can add that it is for particular people that we have 'specific and meaningful, not merely abstract responsibilities of care' (Plumwood 1991: 21). For organization scholars and consultants, this is crucial: one has to analyze and plan for the particular messy reality of people, animals and materialities, and not for the abstract, universal and harmonic unification of everything. This is perhaps part of the reason why neither Plumwood nor Sylvan were involved with political parties, but they were also dismissive of the fact that parties would have to spend time, money and moral principles to be in power (Jackie French, referred to in Hyde 2014: 199). As any oppositional and radical academic would do in the late 1960s and 1970s, they were of course considering anarchism, socialism, Marxism – and the Greens when they came along in Australia in the early 1990s. Sylvan would remain 'an unfashionable anarchist to the end' (Hyde 2014: 141), while Plumwood came to avoid anarchism as a label for her views on how to organize a society at large, being critical of the excessively individualistic elements of anarchism. She came to prefer 'utopian socialist' as a description of her own political position (Hyde 2014: 200). Some readers will find that a turn off, as the label comes heavily loaded with historical baggage. However, by adding utopianism to her socialism, she circumvents the many examples of disastrous manifestations of state socialism in the world. And, of course, she does not shy away from the utopian since certain forms of utopianism are called for in creating new images for organizations. I will not split hairs over labelling, as I find it more interesting to actually see what she says about organizing for an ecological future, in particular as it revolves around the notion of 'bioregionalism'.

In 1993, she talks of bioregionalism as embodying the virtues of friendship, openness to the other, response to others' needs, the expression and recognition of dependency, responsibility and interconnection. 'An important ground of certain caring relations would be a locally particularized identity involving commitment to a particular place and its non-human as well as its human inhabitants' (Plumwood 1993: 186). She is as always worried about authoritarian forms of leadership in bioregions, regions where the political and economic boundaries match the ecological ones. We need democratic processes and involvement from everyone to be able to give agency to nature too. However, she also emphasizes the very real possibility of the emergence of 'shadow places', places that 'provide our material and ecological support, most of which, in a global market, are likely to elude our knowledge and responsibility' (Plumwood 2008: 139. See also Plumwood 2002). This is related to the idea of One True Place that 'commands our identity and loyalty' (Plumwood 2008: 144). Such an attachment to place might turn into the 'national-cultural home', the place elevated above all others, and a discourse producing aliens who are not worthy of dwelling there, aliens coming from places that can be 'deemed degradable' (ibid.: 144). She is tempted to 'swim against the current of the self-sufficiency tide', suggesting a different route, namely, all forms of exchange and responsibility between our place and the places of others. This sounds abstract, and there are indeed many different possibilities for a concretization. For the reader who is interested in the production and trading of food, her own illustration of the complex challenge is of particular relevance. There is a difference between (a) growing one's own vegetables, (b) taking part in a community garden, (c) as a *consumer* supporting agriculture and (d) working in a cooperative for trade justice. So, unity versus dissociation is indeed not her answer. '(A) critical sense of place based on knowledge and care for multiple places could be the form of place consciousness most appropriate to contemporary planetary ecological consciousness' (ibid.: 149). I read this to mean that all of (a–d) are fine as long as we are conscious of what we are doing.

Plumwood's ambivalent affinity with ecofeminism

Plumwood's work is associated with 'ecofeminism', an area of scholarly work and activism embedded in feminism and environmental politics, having its historical roots in the 1970s. The history of ecofeminism depends on the narrator, of course, as the phenomenon has diverse manifestations. Sometimes the concept is used in a very inclusive way, and ecofeminists can then position themselves as 'we who bring feminism and environmentalism together' (MacGregor 2014: 622). Jeffrey Bile suggests that what distinguishes ecofeminism is that the oppression of women and the exploitation of nature are understood as two effects of the same phenomenon. They are not only contingent, but two sides of the same coin: 'Ecofeminism is the belief that coinciding ecological and feminine repressions are often more than coincidental' (Bile 2011: 11). Plumwood's rather pragmatic understanding is that, even if ecological feminism (used interchangeably with 'ecofeminism' by Plumwood) is not one unified position, there is common ground for the different positions: the rejection of the inferiority of women and of nature.

Plumwood was very critical of some positions within ecofeminism in her early work but would also respectfully and systematically build on the work of those she criticized, in order to develop what she calls 'critical ecological feminism' (1993: 1). 'Although much must be rejected', she wrote in 1986, 'what can then be salvaged from ecofeminism is a position which sheds valuable light on the conceptual structure of domination, and makes important critical points about the western philosophical tradition' (Plumwood 1986: 120). She is specific in her critique and opposes positions where women are seen as nature, where the 'false choice' between culture and nature is accepted (Plumwood 1993: 200, fn 16). She is opposed to a 'reversal feminism', feminizing strategies that celebrate women's 'life-giving powers in a way which confirms their immersion in nature' (Plumwood 1993: 31). She is thus clearly opposed to gender 'essentialism' (inborn femininity for women and inborn masculinity for men), but is equally, if not more, critical of those who, in their accusations of essentialism, are not precise in what they are actually criticizing. I would say that she was critically loyal to ecofeminism, as a *critical* ecological feminist would be.

Despite her ambivalence, Plumwood is usually listed among the most important contributors to ecofeminism. She was obviously closely connected to the ecofeminist surge of the 1980s and 1990s – speaking on the same platforms, participating in the same debates, publishing in the same journals as other ecofeminists. And, not least, she was sympathetic to ecofeminism. On the other hand, by the 1980s, Plumwood had already pioneered and positioned herself as a sophisticated deconstructivist by refusing to reverse the gender binary and with a general critique of dualist thinking, as mentioned earlier. She was 'rejecting dualism *per se*' (Sargisson 2001: 59), which sets her apart from most other ecofeminists. I will elaborate a little bit on this.

During the 1980s, the critique of gender essentialism expanded and generated vast amounts of scholarly research. Judith Butler published *Gender Trouble* in 1990 and the book is emblematic of the poststructuralist and deconstructivist turn within gender studies. Even 'benign' forms of gender essentialism were now viewed with suspicion in large parts of the field. Ecofeminism was in general associated with gender reversal politics based on gender essentialism, holding women and femininity as superior to men and masculinity in ecological matters. Val Plumwood was totally in line with the deconstruction of gender from the beginning but was misread by many as an essentialist ecofeminist. Perhaps some of the reason for this was that she took *nature*, not *gender* like Butler, as the fulcrum for her critique of dualist thinking. Plumwood was thus not only marginalized because feminist studies as such are positioned on the fringes of academia. She was also neglected within feminist studies because of the unjust association between her name and the essentialist parts of ecofeminism.

End thoughts

Val Plumwood thinks about nature as oppressed by humans but, unlike most other thinkers on the environment, she consistently thinks about nature as oppressed in relation to other forms of oppression. In the opening of *Feminism and the Mastery of Nature* (1993), she writes:

> It is usually at the edges where great tectonic plates of theory meet and shift that we find the most dramatic developments and upheavals. When four tectonic plates of liberation theory – those concerned with the oppressions of gender, race, class and

nature – finally come together, the resulting tremors could shake the conceptual structures of oppression to their foundations.

(1993: 1)

Her main ideas, some of them developed together with Richard Sylvan, are systematically and thoroughly argued and presented in the book. The tremors can still be felt reading it now in tandem with her subsequent writing. Her conscious reflection and ever-present attention to social and political distinctions like gender, race and class, as well as her philosophy on life and death, makes her work extraordinarily useful for the green global shifts that humans will have to see through. Donna Haraway, whose work perfectly resonates with Plumwood's, writes that '(I)t matters which thoughts think thoughts. We must think!' (Haraway 2016: 57). We could very well let ourselves be inspired by Haraway and Plumwood so that we may creatively contribute to the development of new images and metaphors for how we organize not only how to survive, but how to live well and die well. We must think in imaginative ways and, as far as I can tell, we will have to come up with something quite quickly.

Facts

Valerie Morell, born 11 August 1939.
Valerie Macrae (after marrying John Macrae 1958).
Val Routley (after marrying Francis Richard Routley 1967).
Val Plumwood 1981 (just before divorcing Richard, who after their divorce in 1982 took the name Richard Sylvan).

Published extensively together with Richard as Routley and Routley (e.g. the term 'human chauvinism' was coined by them, evolving from 1973 onwards in papers on circulation (Hyde 2014: 106–107)). They built a stone house in Braidwood, Australia, in a local rainforest on Plumwood Mountain. The plumwood tree had given its name to the mountain. This is also where she died after suffering a stroke on 29 February 2008.

Val had two children from her first marriage; both died young, her daughter under dramatic circumstances and her son of chronic illness.

ANU graduate programme for doctorate March 1982, awarded her PhD April 1991, her thesis was published by Routledge as *Feminism and the Mastery of Nature in* 1993.

Labelled her ideas Critical Ecological Feminism.

Had a series of non-tenured, fixed-term, temporary and casual tutorships and lectureships over the years during her PhD time and after. Would not give up her time at Plumwood Mountain for jobs.

Published single-authored books: *Feminism and the Mastery of Nature* (1993), *Environmental Culture* (2002), *The Eye of the Crocodile* (2012) (posthumously).

Recommended reading

Original text by Val Plumwood

Plumwood, Val (1993) *Feminism and the Mastery of Nature*. London and New York: Routledge.

Key academic text

Hyde, Dominic (2014) *Eco-Logical Lives: The Philosophical Lives of Richard Routley/Sylvan and Val Routley/Sylvan*. Cambridge: White Horse Press.
Phillips, Mary and Rumens, Nick (2016) *Contemporary Perspectives on Ecofeminism*. Oxford and New York: Routledge.

Accessible resource

Griffin, Nicholas (2001) Val Plumwood. In: Palmer Joy A. (ed.): *Fifty Key Thinkers on the Environment*. New York: Taylor & Francis.

Notes

1 Here it must be noted that Plumwood's understanding of the 'natural order' is completely at odds with the understandings held by evolutionary celebrities like the sociobiologist Edward O. Wilson and neo-Darwinist Richard Dawkins, whose ideas she finds to be much lacking. They have a 'mechanistic conception of animals' which they extend to humans, thereby failing to enrich our understanding of the human or the animal (Plumwood 1993: 121–122).
2 To be an ontological vegetarian is to hold it as a fundamental principle not to eat meat. For her, however, there is in principal nothing wrong in eating meat as long as we are ethical and respectful in the way we treat animals. We humans, like all other organisms, have the right to strive to survive. A universal 'ban' on meat is not only culturally arrogant towards those who depend on local meat (hunting, small-scale agricultural production) for fat and protein, but it also implies a new separation between organisms: those worthy of not being eaten, the dignified organisms (animals), and those that can be eaten (plants). We should be grateful and respectful, says Plumwood, towards anything that sustains us, or, as Donna Haraway puts it, we must eat each other 'properly'. This requires that we also *meet* properly (Haraway 2016: 73).
3 It was in the debates between ecofeminists and the philosopher Arne Næss and his theory of 'Deep Ecology' (Næss 1973) that Plumwood developed her main ideas about subjectivity.

References

Bile, Jeffrey 2011. The Rhetorics of Critical Ecofeminism: Conceptual Connection and Reasoned Response. In: Douglas A. Vakoch (ed.): *Ecofeminism and Rhetoric: Critical Perspectives on Sex, Technology and Discourse*. New York and Oxford: Berghahn Books.

Czarniawska, Barbara 2012. New Plots Are Badly Needed in Finance: Accounting for the Financial Crisis of 2007–2010. *Accounting, Auditing and Accountability Journal*, vol. 25, no. 5: 756–775.

Doughty, Caitlin 2015. *Smoke Gets in Your Eyes: And Other Lessons from the Crematory.* New York and London: W.W. Norton & Company.

Doughty, Caitlin 2017. *From Here to Eternity: Traveling the World to Find the Good Death.* New York and London: W.W. Norton & Company.

French, Jackie. 2008. Memories of Val. https://valplumwood.wordpress.com/category/remembering-val-stories-and-obituaries/ (accessed 18 July 2017)

Harari, Yuval Noah 2015 [2011]. *Sapiens: A Brief History of Humankind.* London: Vintage Books.

Haraway, Donna J. 2016. *Staying with the Trouble: Making Kin in the Chthulucene.* Durham, NC and London: Duke University Press.

Hyde, Dominic 2014. *Eco-Logical Lives: The Philosophical Lives of Richard Routley/Sylvan and Val Routley/Sylvan.* Cambridge: White Horse Press.

Lykke, Nina. 2010. *Feminist Studies: A Guide to Intersectional Theory, Methodology and Writing. Routledge Advances in Feminist Studies and Intersectionality.* New York and London: Routledge.

MacGregor, Sherilyn 2014. Only Resist: Feminist Ecological Citizenship and the Post-politics of Climate Change. *Hypatia* vol. 29, no. 3 (Summer): 617–633.

Morgan, Gareth 2006. *Images of Organizations: Updated Edition of the International Bestseller.* Thousand Oaks, CA, London, and New Delhi: Sage.

Morgan, Gareth 2016. Commentary: Beyond Morgan's Eight Metaphors. *Human Relations*, vol. 69, no. 4: 1029–1042.

Næss, Arne 1973. The Shallow and the Deep, Long-range Ecology Movement. *Inquiry*, vol. 16: 95–100.

Plumwood, Val 1986. Ecofeminism: An Overview and Discussion of Positions and Arguments. *Australasian Journal of Philosophy*, Supplement to vol. 64: June, 120–138.

Plumwood, Val 1991. Nature, Self and Gender: Feminism, Environmental Philosophy and the Critique of Rationalism. *Hypatia*, vol. 6, no. 1 (Spring): 3–25.

Plumwood, Val 1993. *Feminism and the Mastery of Nature.* London and New York: Routledge.

Plumwood, Val 1996. Being Prey. *Terra Nova*, vol. 1, no. 3 (Summer): 32–44.

Plumwood, Val 1999. Being Prey. In: D. Rothenberg and M. Ulveus (eds.): *The New Earth Reader: The Best of Terra Nova.* Cambridge, MA: MIT Press: 76–99. Revised version printed as the chapter 'Meeting the Predator' in Plumwood 2012: 9–21. For an account of other printed versions, see Hyde 2014: 16. Can also be downloaded at: http://institut-kunst.ch/wp-content/uploads/2016/05/Plumwood_Being-Prey.pdf (accessed 13 July 2017).

Plumwood, Val 2002. *Environmental Culture: The Ecological Crisis of Reason.* London: Routledge.

Plumwood, Val 2007. The Cemetery Wars: Cemeteries, Biodiversity and the Sacred. *Local-Global: Identity, Security and Community*, Vol. 3. Special issue: Exploring the legacy of Judith Wright, eds. Martin Mulligan and Yaso Nadarajah: 54–71.

Plumwood, Val 2008. Shadow Places and the Politics of Dwelling. *Australian Humanities Review*, 44 (March): 139–150.

Plumwood, Val 2012. *The Eye of the Crocodile*. Edited by Lorraine Shannon. Canberra: ANU E Press.

Salmon, Jane 2008. Story of the Burial of Val Plumwood. http://studylib.net/doc/7573260/story-of-the-burial-of-val-plumwood (accessed 13 July 2017).

Sargisson, Lucy 2001. What's Wrong with Ecofeminism? *Environmental Politics*, vol. 10, no. 1: 52–64.

4 Contributions from Gayatri C. Spivak to organizational thinking

Rethinking identity, ethics and responsibility in a global context

Banu Özkazanç-Pan

Gayatri C. Spivak is an Indian-born scholar and philosopher whose main areas of scholarship are at the intersections of English literature, feminist theory and postcoloniality. Here, postcoloniality refers broadly to the study of the ways in which colonial powers, such as France, Britain and Spain, impacted the economies and societies of colonized nations and people. Spivak is currently Professor of Humanities at Columbia University and co-founder of the Institute for Comparative Literature and Society. Born in 1942 in Calcutta, India, Spivak spent the majority of her intellectual life in institutions in Europe and the United States (for an overview of Spivak's early career, see Abdalkafor, 2015). Her work has had a major influence on the trajectory of postcolonial studies as a field of inquiry on/about the 'Third World' or as she suggests, what was left of the world after the United States and Russia split it up. In all, the multitude of contributions of Spivak to literature, feminist theories, and postcolonial studies are wide-ranging in their subject matter but share a commonality in influencing significantly the kinds of analyses that were being done in academia in relation to the Third World/Global South and specifically South East Asia. It has been difficult to pinpoint Spivak, throughout her career, as belonging to a particular intellectual tradition given the range of theories she deployed to craft arguments and engage in analyses.

Despite this observation, Spivak's major contributions to the field of postcolonial studies arrive from her engagement with the concept of the subaltern through feminist and deconstructive lenses, her use of the concept of 'strategic essentialism' and her consideration of the 'Other' as an epistemic analytic category for discussions around textual representation and voice. In the next section, I discuss her intellectual contributions in more detail and focus on key concepts, namely the *subaltern*, 'strategic essentialism', and 'Other', arriving out of her complex analytic lenses. While these concepts may seem rather abstract, here I offer some clarity and definitions around them. Next, I expand upon these points and provide their applications in organization studies.

Subaltern generally refers to those low-wage, low-status workers in the Third World/Global South that exist beyond the existing structures of society. Thus, subaltern is a way to speak about people who are generally not considered by privileged intellectuals or formal theories in terms of their location with respect to institutions, the economy, society and organizations broadly. Spivak's earlier engagement with the concept suggested that those in a subaltern state could not speak or, essentially, their very existence was beyond formal political, economic and social structures of societies. Put differently, there were no words or ideas to represent the experiences of the subaltern or speak for/about them. In her later works, she spoke about subaltern as a position that had some agency in speaking for/about themselves but in terms that may not have been recognizable by the West and Western intellectuals. One cannot call him/herself a subaltern because they occupy a minority or oppressed position in the West – rather, this is a subject position reserved for those experiences under colonialism beyond our elite intellectual view and understanding of the world.

Strategic essentialism speaks to the intentional use of categories, such as women, as analytic tools to speak to conditions of life and work under global capitalism. By using this concept, Spivak engages with the possibility for change that comes about when individuals strategically and carefully use categories to speak about issues that transverse national boundaries and bind people together. It is a way to speak about and examine shared conditions in life despite differences across dimensions, identities and politics.

The *Other* is a concept that allows scholars to uncover assumptions guiding Western ideas about cultural others – for example, notions of what women's experiences must be like in non-Western contexts; ideas about values and attitudes of people who do not share the same ethnicity or religion in nations beyond the West; assumptions about the ways in which people live and work in societies that do not resemble one's own. Together, these ideas become texts or ways of speaking about, thinking about and writing about people in the world that the West does not readily recognize as 'progressive'. In many ways, the Other is a way to speak back to assumptions about the Third World and particularly women in these contexts as needing 'help' or aid from the West. These assumptions do not allow for understanding the experiences, skills or knowledge of people that are different but rather deemed 'backwards' or traditional.

To contextualize these contributions to postcolonial and feminist scholarship, understanding Spivak's early career is useful particularly given the influence that certain intellectual traditions had on her development. In the 1980s, Spivak worked as part of the Subaltern Studies, a group of South East Asian scholars interested in examining the consequences of colonialism, particularly in the Indian context. Guided by the mentorship of Ranajit Guha and others, this group was influenced heavily by the work of Antonio Gramsci, an Italian theorist and politician jailed for his ideas about elites, capitalism and hegemony. Gramsci used the notion of *subalterno* or the subaltern to suggest people that were left out of their own societies by wealthy, capitalist elites who used culture, consent and institutions to keep their dominance and power over the population. The Subaltern Studies Group aimed to provide a critical history of South East Asia and used this notion of subaltern to demonstrate how coloniality was a forgotten analytic component and material condition of Marxist historiography (see Guha and Spivak, 1988).

Here, Marxist historiography refers to those scholars of history and economics that use the economic and political theories of Karl Marx (and Friedrich Engels) to explain the development of economies, societies and nations. One of Marx's hallmark contributions was his theory about class struggles between the working class and capitalists, who owned the means of production (i.e. factories, businesses, land) under capitalism. Marx believed that in societies where such struggles were taking shape, communism would eventually overtake capitalism. The Subaltern Studies Group believed that such theories about economic development were linear and did not speak to the detrimental role of colonialism in the march towards communism. For Marx, colonialism was simply a transitory step towards communism and did little to acknowledge or theorize its decimation of societies. Within the Subaltern Studies Group, Spivak focused on developing the notion of the subaltern beyond Gramsci's engagement to include those colonized people that were beyond the Western gaze and beyond history's analytic categories, existing under conditions that could not be recognized through contemporary capitalism. In many ways, subaltern became an analytic category that spoke about those groups of people who had been left out of Marxist analysis and out of history in the context of South East Asia.

In all, Spivak's concepts of subaltern, strategic essentialism and the Other also capture and address issues related to agency and structure – a point that is relevant to her analyses about gendered and racialized labour in the context of globalization. While not representing the entirety of her scholarship, these concepts are foundational to her analyses derived from postcolonial, Marxist, deconstructionist and feminist philosophies. Guided by these concepts, the focus of this chapter is on how her interdisciplinary work and scholarship provide new directions for organizational thinking and the nexus of business and society. Specifically, I focus on contributions available from Spivak's scholarship to notions of subjectivity, ethics and corporate governance in the context of globalization. Taken together, Gayatri Spivak's intellectual contributions are well-poised to expand upon the repertoire of organizational theorizing that has long been dominated by masculinist paradigms that are not only blind to gender as an organizing principle of organizational life and society but also unrepresentative of the different experiences and views emanating from non-Western traditions and experiences.

Intellectual contributions

In general, postcoloniality has had a critical engagement with representations of the Third World/ Global South 'Other' in the Western discourse and text (Said, 1983, 1993/2012). Put more succinctly, it is 'a radical rethinking of knowledge and social identities authored and authorized by colonialism and Western domination' (Prakash, 1994: 1475). The subaltern project aimed to speak about/to the 'Third World' subject that had been denied agency in Marxist, colonialist and nationalist discourse of the West as well as in the literature and social imaginary of Europe (Prakash, 1994; Said, 1978). Spivak further expanded upon these analyses as she advanced the subaltern concept to discuss both the subject of representation in such texts but also to outline possibilities for agency. In brief, postcoloniality arising out of Subaltern Studies has been the predominant form of critique in academic circles vis-a-vis the engagement of the Global North with the Third World/Global South despite the fact that colonial histories in Latin America and the Pacific differ in their nature and form colonial experiences in the 'Orient' and South East Asia.

One of Spivak's best-known contributions to postcolonial studies in her engagement with the concept of the subaltern and subalternity more broadly (Spivak, 1988a). Developed from Gramsci's *subalterno*, which as a concept focused on those groups of people who were written out of history and societal institutions, subaltern was defined by the Subaltern Studies Group explicitly in relation to coloniality (El Louai, 2012). In this sense, the project of the Subaltern Studies Group was to expand upon those material conditions that were necessarily but unspoken in Marx's conceptual framework or historiography. In moving from feudalism to capitalism, Marx's notion of change did not allow for consideration of agency in the subjects that would now be rules under different economic regimes. By re-theorizing and re-engaging with these concepts, the Subaltern Studies Group aimed to provide a different theory of change, one that specifically addressed concerns around agency in the 'Third-World' subject or the subaltern.

As Chakrabarty states, 'Subaltern historiography necessarily entailed (*a*) a relative separation of the history of power from any universalist histories of capital, (*b*) a critique of the nation-form, and (*c*) an interrogation of the relationship between power and knowledge (hence of the archive itself and of history as a form of knowledge)' (2000: 15). Further, there was an attempt to reconsider the role of politics and power 'from below' in examining the role of peasant rebellions as examples of such horizontal mobilizations deploying networks of kin while vertical mobilizations by elites used formal institutions (Chakrabarty, 2000; Guha, 1988). For Spivak, this change was not a transition but a violent rupture better characterized as 'confrontations' as well as a significant change in the 'sign-systems' or those appellations associated with the changes in the economic system (Spivak, 1988b: 3). To clarify, Spivak focused on those groups of people who existed in the lowest levels of society and rebelled or confronted the changes taking shape – subaltern was the conceptual space that she deployed to theorize about these subjects who were centrally impacted by the material changes taking shape in the economy and political sphere. Fundamentally, the intersections of nationalism and capitalism as moments of historic change in India provided the impetus for re-theorizing historiography from a subaltern lens.

Spivak further developed the subaltern concept as an analytic lens to focus on the 'Third-World' female subject in history and in Western texts and is emblematic of her use of Marxist *and* deconstructionist approaches simultaneously. One of the main concerns she outlines through the use of this concept is related to the social imaginary as exemplified in the 'Other' of Europe. She states, 'it is impossible for French intellectuals [such as Foucault] to imagine the kind of Power and Desire that would inhabit the unnamed subject of the Other of Europe' (Spivak 1988a: 280). Thus, Spivak engages in both a material and discursive analysis in relation to the subaltern, meaning that she examines the ways in which particular organizational practices lead to consequences for Third World workers *and* the ways in which such people are understood in the West through media representations, scholarly work and writing. Using both these approaches, she demonstrates the intersections of gendered, racialized labour power with changes in the sign-system whereby the location of agency becomes situated in the very subject who was deemed to be outside of capital flows. In other words, Spivak allows the subaltern to occupy an important position in any analysis pertaining to organizational and economic activities in postcolonial contexts.

I expand upon these points in the context of organization studies to provide insights about new possibilities for rethinking extant notions of identity/representation, ethics and inequality. Specifically, Spivak's engagement with epistemology/knowledge production, representation and voice allows revisiting traditional concepts and subjects associated with contemporary organizational thinking in relation to how we represent and identify people. Further, her engagement with strategic essentialism as well as subalternity allows scholars to consider who speaks for whom and for what in organizational contexts. Following this discussion, I focus on subjectivity as a way to understand and know subjects, an ethical proposition that lends itself rethinking business ethics beyond deontology. This has implications for our conceptualizations of corporate social responsibility (CSR). Finally, Spivak's concepts allow renewed focus on inequality as an organizing principle of societies and its reflections in the very ways organizations may rely and require it as they conduct their affairs across the globe. Specifically, the gendered and racialized division of labour underpins much of business today, yet organization studies have yet to sufficiently examine its own complicity in ignoring this fact and potentially perpetuating such labour conditions under the guise of 'good' international business strategy: outsourcing business production and services to low-wage laborers across the globe.

Contributions to organization studies

Identity and representation: concerns over epistemology and agency

In translating the possibilities of postcolonial concepts and issues to organization studies, there has been a growing and rich tradition of postcolonial work challenging dominant managerialist ideologies based on Western humanism and worldviews more generally (Banerjee and Prasad, 2008; Jack et al., 2011; Özkazanç-Pan, 2008; Prasad, 2003,

2012). These include engagement with notions of hybridity (Frenkel and Shenhav, 2006; Yousfi, 2014), post- and anti-colonial reading of African leadership (Nkomo, 2011), examining the use of English in call centres (Boussebaa, Sinha, and Gabriel, 2014) and examining the production of Whiteness in expatriates living in postcolonial contexts (Leonard, 2016).

In all, these and other works that deploy postcolonial lenses call attention to the intersections of epistemic claims made by and in organizational theory about the 'Other' – despite the importance and relevance of these works, there is less attention given to issues at the intersection of postcoloniality and gender with notable exceptions (Calás and Smircich, 2006; Holvino, 2010; Özkazanç-Pan, 2012). Yet there are many more possibilities for rethinking issues of identity and representation if the work of Spivak is expanded upon to engage these concepts.

To this end, her work on epistemic claims and 'epistemic violence' whereby subaltern knowledge and ways of being in the world become effaced by dominant ideologies and discourses of the West speak directly to issues of identity and representation. Static notions of identity that arrive from Western psychological concepts guide much of organizational theorizing in relation to cultural 'Others' (Özkazanç-Pan and Calás, 2015). Yet postcolonial notions of identity require engagement with notions of epistemology and agency – in other words, postcoloniality does not necessarily offer alternative notions of identity but rather, questions the very epistemology of identity claims that simultaneously imbue agency in Western individuals but vacate such agency in the context of the Third World, particularly in relation to women (Mohanty, 1988; Mohanty, Russo, and Torres, 1991).

Beyond providing a new or alternative way to conceptualize identity as is the case with other postcolonial thinkers, such as Bhabha's notion of hybridity (Bhabha, 1994), Spivak's analytic framework requires considering identity and identity claims in conjunction with notions of epistemology and agency – thus, identity is not a concept describing one's self but rather an epistemic claiming of a self in relation to Others. This act of claiming requires the erasure of possibility for those deemed Other such that any attempt at 'speaking back' or 'speaking about' oneself from a position of Other requires vacating a subject position deemed to have no agency. The problematic of this position is that those worldviews and notions of self that arrive from non-Western traditions must be explained in order to gain legitimacy in a space, such as Western texts about management or organization, that already places it in an epistemologically inferior position. To claim to speak for oneself from a position of postcoloniality is already an act of defiance of the epistemic rules governing Western psychological concepts of self and becoming (Bhatia and Ram, 2001, 2009).

Spivak's work allows us to consider how claiming identity is an ethico-political act that arrives out of defying the rules of the epistemic game – a concern about whether subaltern subjects are spoken for and about yet rarely afforded agency in Western texts. In all, these concerns challenge us to reconsider how theory and research about the Third World may silence its subjects and to consider ethical dimensions about the very production of research on/about management and organizations in the context of the Global South/Third World. These concerns lead to the next contribution that arrives out of Spivak's core concepts – that of ethics as the possibility of agency versus a normative or deontological set of guidelines around how people and businesses should behave.

Ethics

One of Spivak's main concerns is the ethico-political dimension of knowledge production about the Third World/Global South and the consequences of such knowledge for the working lives of laborers, a point I expand upon in the next section. Yet ethics arriving out of postcoloniality is not a set of guidelines about what to do and how to do it, particularly in the context of organizations. That is, ethics is the possibility of imbuing agency in the Third World subject in organizational texts when much of such writing effaces the voices and experiences of such subjects (Ibarra-Colado, 2006; Kwek 2003). Expanding further on this point, Spivak's focus on Third World women in particular requires rethinking ethics as an engagement with the consequences of knowledge production *and* the material consequences. In other words, ethics is not an abstraction, but an affording of agency in the moment of encounter between people. Or as she suggests, 'this [ethical] encounter can only happen when the respondent inhabits something like normality' (Spivak, 1995: xxv).

This notion of ethics stands in stark contrast to our understanding of 'the right thing to do' particularly in the context of organizational life and the intersections of business and society. If normative/deontological approaches to business ethics requires a set of guidelines around behaviour, then postcolonial engagement with ethics derived from Spivak requires a conversation about responsibility and accountability in the context of agency. That is, agency is central to the theory and practice of ethics, which in turn relates back to how we speak about and engage the 'Other' in our organizational theorizing and research. The recognition and responding to the subaltern is the enactment of ethics. Spivak states this clearly in the following: 'When the subaltern "speaks" in order to be heard and gets into the structure of responsible (responding and being responded to) resistance, he or she is or is on the way to becoming an organic intellectual' (1995: xxvi).

In relating these notions of ethics to organization studies, we can focus on two interrelated issues: how we theorize ethics and how we theorize the ethical subject. Theorizing ethics in the context of organizational life and organizational studies more broadly involves a rethinking of the constitution and role of business in society – how do the ways in which we understand norms of behaviour at the individual or organizational level arrive from assumptions derived from Western epistemologies. And how might such assumptions be challenged so as to open up textual and epistemic space to include those notions of 'ethics' that are derived from views of the world that are fundamentally different in their ontological notions of reality, such as Confucius or Islamic teachings as examples. For example, the nature of the social world and human existence are theorized fundamentally in different ways under Confucius thought – in this sense, the role of humans is not to dominate the earth but to live in harmony. Organizing for societal harmony as an ethical principle of business is strikingly different than organizing for profit-making. As a consequence, what is considered an ethical organization or an ethical way to do business will be different based on one's assumptions about the nature of the social world and our place in it. Similarly, Islamic teachings encompass the totality of one's life rather than fragment them – consequently, there is no separation between personal ethics and business ethics given that such a dichotomy does not make sense for those practicing Islam. In this example, ethics speaks to how one lives life and practices their beliefs rather than resorting to a context-specific set of actions.

Following these examples and related to the ways in which actors and actions can be understood, traditional notions of (business) ethics generally espouse an abstract individual as the foundation for theorizing (organizational) behaviour. Yet Spivak offers subaltern agency as a simultaneous problematic of choice and structure specifically in the organizational contexts. Through subaltern agency as a guiding lens, how might we rethink ethics and our understanding of ethical organizational behaviour? As one example, scholars can consider how structures of authority and hierarchy coupled with neo-liberal ideologies provide the foundation for what is considered appropriate and ethical behaviour in organizational contexts. In contrast, a relational and contextual understanding of ethics can emerge that moves it beyond the current abstract individualism. Or alternative philosophies, such as the ones mentioned above, provide further depth and nuance to 'business ethics' as an ever-shifting concept. Moving beyond this contribution, Spivak's work lays the foundation for a questioning and redirecting of appropriate corporate behaviour in a global context or corporate governance and social responsibility.

While extant theorizing on corporate social responsibility (CSR) including critical engagements and political CSR, Spivak's work allows reframing the conversation by linking epistemology and materiality as necessary to conceptualizing corporate action in a globally interconnected context. To this end, her simultaneous focus on text and materiality can prove fruitful to consider epistemic violence in regards to the low-wage, low-status gendered subject of CSR. In other words, how should we think and write about the women who work for very little pay in conditions that are considered illegal in most Western nations? Spivak's focus on the material conditions of such workers highlights the role of corporations in governance and structural arrangements globally – how should we think about corporations that outsource work to nations where there are few regulations around labour and the environment and the majority of workers are young women? How might organizational scholars and scholarship attend to these issues at the core of their theories? By bringing together epistemic and material engagement to theorizing CSR (Özkazanç-Pan, 2018), Spivak's work can highlight the complexity of corporate action as well as the possibilities for change. Her work compels us to ask difficult questions, such as 'who is responsible for the living and work conditions faced by millions of South East Asian women labourers producing goods for wealthy Western and other nations?' In other words, Spivak's concepts force us to rethink 'business ethics' when the very ways of doing business under capitalism by using low-wage, low-status workers are, in fact, by their nature unethical.

Expanding further on what might be different about ethics if we open up opportunities from postcoloniality, an additional consideration would be the difference between teaching ethics and teaching ethically (Kweder and Özkazanç-Pan, 2015). In other words, if the forms and content of knowledge diffused in business schools obfuscates its ideological basis, neo-liberalism to be precise, then what might acknowledging these assumptions make a difference in how and what we teach our students. Only recently have conversations around the importance of people and planet in addition to profit become embedded in the MBA curriculum and business schools more broadly – yet postcoloniality and other critical traditions have already examined these issues much more in-depth and thus stand to provide important contributions about how the structuring of society and the economy in various contexts can lead to the perpetuation of inequalities (for example, see Banerjee, 2003).

It is these kinds of observations and engagements that provide opportunity for re-thinking ethics in the context of organization studies – should our inability to address these issues as scholars and educators be the fundamental ethical lapse that has laid the foundations for the inequalities and corruption that we have seen take shape in corporate contexts? To examine the issue of inequality and how postcoloniality can contribute to our inclusion of it in our research agendas and theories, I expand upon the intersections of inequality and labour guided by Spivak's focused on the gendered, racialized division of global labour.

Inequality and labour

One of Spivak's hallmark contributions is her complex analysis around the division of labour in the global interconnected economies of the world. Derived from Marxist, deconstructionist and gender-focused analytics, Spivak has long focused on the ways in which the gendered subaltern functions within the context of neo-liberalism particularly after 'nationalism' in her native India. Her analysis has examined the ways in which the labour is extracted from such groups of people and the implications of such extraction for our understanding of value. Here, she expands our notions of value beyond the economic to consider the ethics of valuing certain groups of people less as if they are less human. Spivak's incisive analysis points us in the direction of inequality, which can be defined beyond the economic and material conditions one is forced to labour under to include those discursive forms that position the subaltern as the 'Other' who is somehow below the West and local elites in non-Western contexts. This dehumanizing aspect of value extraction speaks to what we traditionally call inequality.

Yet, organization studies have barely scratched the surface in examining inequality as an organizing principle of society and the economy, meaning that inequality organizes our experiences of society, organizations and everyday life. This is unfortunate given that fields such as sociology, women's studies and anthropology have made significant progress in examining the structures, mechanisms and contexts related to the production and replication of various kinds of inequalities including economic and gender-based ones (Acker, 2006; Tomaskovic-Devey, 1993; Tomaskovic-Devey and Skaggs, 2002).

Postcolonial contributions to organization studies can speak directly to such inequalities in historic context (see Khan, Munir, and Wilmott, 2007). Thus, while there is some interest in examining inequality recently in the organization studies field (Riaz, 2015), there is much more that needs to be mainstreamed.

While the majority of organization studies and management scholars have not examined inequality in relation to their scholarship, there are noteworthy exceptions that have deployed postcolonial lenses to examine such issues, including their examination in the context of gender and entrepreneurship (Özkazanç-Pan, 2014) and in relation to organization studies more broadly (Calás and Smircich, 2006; Zanoni et al., 2010). In doing so, these scholars have highlighted the relevance of both discursive and material aspects of inequality across gender dimensions. Deriving specifically from Spivak's work, further research can focus on the ways global production networks required gendered and racialized labour of the Global South for the production of goods that are consumed by developed nations, including those in the Global North.

Further to this point, Spivak's analytic framework around the role of discursive alongside the material can be used to examine how gender-based development efforts in postcolonial nations under the umbrella of public–private partnerships (PPPs) may locate agency and 'empowerment' in individual women rather than dismantling structures of inequality. Some critical work in this regard can be seen in relation to the outcomes of microfinance in South East Asia. Scholars note that while such efforts claim to be empowering women, they do little to change gender relations in society (Hunt and Kasynathan, 2001). Rather, an analysis that underscores the role of development efforts of nation-states in postcolonial context through a gender lens is necessary in order to understand the interrelated aspects of inequality and how they become replicated is necessary (see McClintock, Mufti, and Shohat, 1997).

Organizational scholarship plays an important role in highlighting the role of organizations in addressing such inequalities and potentially challenging them given that the very activities of corporate entities in the Global South can be the source of inequalities in the first place (Marens, 2013). To this end, understanding the role that organizations play in the context of societal level structures and cultural norms and psychological level biases can yield insights about the working lives and experiences of subaltern laborers. Yet such discursive and material considerations rarely represent the majority of mainstream organizational scholarship, whereby the research paradigm still focuses on 'implications for managers' or 'for doing business internationally'. Rather, the role and complicity of organizations in perpetuating gendered global capitalism (see to Calás et al., 2010) are not the main focus of organization studies. To this end, Spivak's framework provides much nuance and rigour to existing analyses of organizational life and organizations more broadly in a global context.

The future

Spivak's lens provides much analytic depth for rethinking the Euro-centric philosophical underpinnings of organizational theories and theorizing. As we enter a transnational phase of human migration where new and old diasporas are made and remade (Spivak, 1996), the role of organizations particularly in the context of the Global South increasingly need careful analysis and examination. In many ways, the increasing use of PPPs in the name of development in transition and Global South nations have resulted in the heralding of women's empowerment through neo-liberal ideologies and actions, such as entrepreneurship. The role-gendered global capitalism in extracting labour from the subaltern needs to play a central role in how we theorize organizations in contemporary societies. Yet the current political climate in the United States and in other nations where alt-right, anti-immigrant rhetoric has become normalized makes critical theories and theorizing even more important despite the potential for backlash. In such times, postcolonial frameworks stand to articulate and elucidate the dangerous intersections of nationalism and gendered capitalism as particular groups become 'Others' in their own nations.

What role can and should organizations play when they stand to impact the working lives of millions of people globally and how should organization scholars attend to these issues in their research and writing? While scholars may not be in a position to impact the actions of large corporate actors, we are in a position to educate organizational leaders, managers and others who should be imparted a set of skills and lenses to understand the complexity of the world – yet not in a way that obscures the neo-liberal underpinnings of business scholarship but rather one that highlights these assumptions and challenges them. Postcolonial theorizing provides insights about how assumptions about cultural 'Others' and actions taken on their behalf run counter to self-proclaimed democracies and create false hierarchies in societies. Issues of identity/representation in relation to agency and voice are hallmark considerations of Spivak's postcolonial lens – they offer us the ability to rethink what constitutes empowerment in the context of socioeconomic, cultural and political structures which produce/replicate inequality. Further, by focusing on ethics as the possibility of agency, Spivak's work pushes our notions of business ethics beyond normative guidelines and towards the political dimensions of theorizing the 'Other' as a full person, a human, an equal. Finally, Spivak's analysis of the intersections of gender and race in the context of globalized capitalism and subaltern labour provide insights about the role of business and organizations more broadly in shaping societies. The growing movement of people across borders out of choice or force requires us to adopt theoretical frameworks that can attend to power relations and historical processes in the making and remaking of societies. These societal changes have implications for the interrelated ways organizations and societies influence each other and in turn, for the ways these changes impact inequalities across relations of gender, race, ethnicity and so forth. In all, Spivak's work provides much needed critical perspective derived from the intersections of gender and postcolonial analysis to the field of organization studies and offers scholars the required concepts and language to critique extant assumptions of the field and move it forward.

Recommended reading

Original text by Spivak

Spivak, G. C. (2012). *In Other Worlds: Essays in Cultural Politics*. London: Routledge.

Key academic text

Landry, D. and Maclean, G. (1996). *The Spivak Reader*. London: Routledge.

Accessible resource

Morton, S. (2007). *Gayatri Spivak*. Cambridge: Polity Press.

References

Abdalkafor, O. (2015). *Gayatri Spivak: Deconstruction and the Ethics of Postcolonial Literary Interpretation*. Newcastle upon Tyne, UK: Cambridge Scholars Publishing.

Acker, J. (2006). Inequality regimes: Gender, class, and race in organizations. *Gender & Society*, 20(4): 441–464.

Banerjee, S. B. (2003). Who sustains whose development? Sustainable development and the reinvention of nature. *Organization Studies*, 24(1): 143–180.

Banerjee, S. B., and Prasad, A. (2008). Introduction to the special issue on 'Critical reflections on management and organizations: A postcolonial perspective'. *Critical Perspectives on International Business*, 4(2/3): 90–98.

Bhabha, H. (1994). *The Location of Culture*. New York: Routledge.

Bhatia, S., and Ram, A. (2001). Rethinking 'acculturation' in relation to diasporic cultures and postcolonial identities. *Human Development*, 44(1): 1–18.

Bhatia, S., and Ram, A. (2009). Theorizing identity in transnational and diaspora cultures: A critical approach to acculturation. *International Journal of Intercultural Relations*, 33(2): 140–149.

Boussebaa, M., Sinha, S., & Gabriel, Y. (2014). Englishization in offshore call centers: A postcolonial perspective. *Journal of International Business Studies*, 45(9): 1152–1169.

Calás, M. B., and Smircich, L. (2006) 'From the "woman's' point of view"' ten years later: Towards a feminist organization studies. In S. R. Clegg, C. Hardy, T. B. Lawrence and W. L. Nord (Eds.), *The Sage Handbook of Organization Studies*, 2nd ed., pp. 284–346. Thousand Oaks, CA: Sage.

Calás, M. B., Smircich, L., Tienari, J., and Ellehave, C. F. (2010). Observing globalized capitalism: Gender and ethnicity as an entry point. *Gender, Work & Organization*, 17(3): 243–247.

Chakrabarty, D. (2000). Subaltern studies and postcolonial historiography. *Nepantla: Views from the South*, 1(1): 9–32.

El Louai, H. (2012). Retracing the concept of the subaltern from Gramsci to Spivak: Historical developments and new applications. *African Journal of History and Culture*, 4(1): 4–8.

Frenkel, M., and Shenhav, Y. (2006). From binarism back to hybridity: A postcolonial reading of management and organization studies. *Organization Studies*, 27(6): 855–876.

Guha, R. (1988). On some aspects of the historiography of colonial India. In R. Guha and G. C. Spivak (Eds.), *Selected Subaltern Studies*, pp. 37–44. Oxford: Oxford University Press.

Guha, R., and Spivak, G. C. (Eds.). (1988). *Selected Subaltern Studies*. New York: Oxford University Press.

Holvino, E. (2010). Intersections: The simultaneity of race, gender and class in organization studies. *Gender, Work & Organization*, 17(3): 248–277.

Hunt, J., and Kasynathan, N. (2001). Pathways to empowerment? Reflections on microfinance and transformation in gender relations in South Asia. *Gender & Development*, 9(1): 42–52.

Ibarra-Colado, E. (2006). Organization studies and epistemic coloniality in Latin America: Thinking otherness from the margins. *Organization*, 13(4): 463–488.

Jack, G., Westwood, R. I., Srinivas, N., and Sardar, Z. (2011). Deepening, broadening and re-asserting a postcolonial interrogative space in organization studies. *Organization*, 18(3): 275–302.

Khan, F. R., Munir, K. A., and Willmott, H. (2007). A dark side of institutional entrepreneurship: Soccer balls, child labour and postcolonial impoverishment. *Organization Studies*, 28(7): 1055–1077.

Kweder, M. A., and Özkazanç-Pan, B. (2015). From teaching ethics to ethical teaching: Feminist interventions in management education. In *Gender Equality: A Challenge for Management Education UN PRME*. Sheffield: Greenleaf.

Kwek, D. (2003). Decolonizing and re-presenting culture's consequences: A postcolonial critique of cross-cultural studies in management. In A. Prasad (Ed.), *Postcolonial Theory and Organizational Analysis: A Critical Engagement*, pp. 121–146. New York: Palgrave Macmillan.

Leonard, P. (2016). *Expatriate Identities in Postcolonial Organizations: Working Whiteness*. Routledge, NY.

Marens, R. 2013. Calling in a debt: Government's role in creating the capacity for explicit corporate social responsibility. *Business and Society Review*, 118(2): 143–169.

McClintock, A., Mufti, A., and Shohat, E. (Eds.). (1997). *Dangerous Liaisons: Gender, Nation, and Postcolonial Perspectives* (Vol. 11). Minneapolis, MN: University of Minnesota Press.

Mohanty, C. T. (1988). Under Western eyes: Feminist scholarship and colonial discourses. *Feminist Review*, 30: 61–88.

Mohanty, C. T., Russo, A., & Torres, L. (Eds.). (1991). *Third World Women and the Politics of Feminism* (Vol. 632). Bloomington, IN Indiana University Press.

Nkomo, S. M. (2011). A postcolonial and anti-colonial reading of 'African' leadership and management in organization studies: Tensions, contradictions and possibilities. *Organization*, 18(3): 365–386.

Özkazanç-Pan, B. (2008). International management meets 'the rest of the world'. *Academy of Management Review*, 33(4): 964–974.

Özkazanç-Pan, B. (2012). Postcolonial feminist research: Challenges and complexities. *Equality, Diversity and Inclusion: An International Journal*, 31(5/6): 573–591.

Özkazanç-Pan, B. (2014). Postcolonial feminist analysis of high-technology entrepreneuring. *International Journal of Entrepreneurial Behaviour and Research*, 20(2): 155–172.

Özkazanç-Pan, B. (2018). CSR as gendered neocoloniality in the Global South. *Journal of Business Ethics*. doi:10.1007/s10551-018-3798-1, http://rdcu.be/F0FP

Özkazanç-Pan, B., and Calás, M. B. (2015). Transnational approaches to diversity. In R. Bendl, I. Bleijenbergh, E. Henttonen, and A. Mills (Eds.), *The Oxford Handbook of Diversity*, pp. 376–390. Oxford: Oxford University Press.

Prakash, G. (1994). Subaltern studies as postcolonial criticism. *The American Historical Review*, 99(5): 1475–1490.

Prasad, A. (2003). *Postcolonial Theory and Organizational Analysis: A Critical Engagement*. London: Springer.

Prasad, A. (Ed.). (2012). *Against the Grain: Advances in Postcolonial Organization Studies* (Vol. 28). Copenhagen: Copenhagen Business School Press DK.

Riaz, S. (2015). Bringing inequality back in: The economic inequality footprint of management and organizational practices. *Human Relations*, 68(7): 1085–1097.

Said, E. W. (1983). *The World, the Text, and the Critic*. Cambridge, MA: Harvard University Press.

Said, E. W. (1978). *Orientalism.* New York: Random House.
Said, E. W. (1993/2012). *Culture and Imperialism.* New York: Vintage.
Spivak, G. C. (1988a). Can the subaltern speak? Reflections on the history of an idea. In C. Nelson and L. Grossberg (Eds.), *Marxism and the Interpretation of Culture,* pp. 271–314. Chicago, IL: University of Illinois Press.
Spivak, G. C. (1988b). Deconstructing historiography. In R. Guha and G. C. Spivak (Eds.). *Selected Subaltern Studies,* pp. 3–34. Oxford: Oxford University Press.
Spivak, G. C. (1995). *Imaginary Maps: Three Stories by Mahasweta Devi.* New York: Routledge.
Spivak, G. C. (1996). Diasporas old and new: Women in the transnational world. *Textual Practice,* 10(2): 245–269.
Tomaskovic-Devey, D. (1993). *Gender & racial inequality at work: The sources and consequences of job segregation* (No. 27). Ithaca, NY: Cornell University Press.
Tomaskovic-Devey, D., & Skaggs, S. (2002). Sex segregation, labor process organization, and gender earnings inequality. *American Journal of Sociology,* 108(1): 102–128.
Yousfi, H. (2014). Rethinking hybridity in postcolonial contexts: What changes and what persists? The Tunisian case of Poulina's managers. *Organization Studies,* 35(3): 393–421.
Zanoni, P., Janssens, M., Benschop, Y., and Nkomo, S. (2010). Guest editorial: Unpacking diversity, grasping inequality: Rethinking difference through critical perspectives. *Organization,* 17(1): 9–29.

5 Lauren Berlant

Cruel organizations

Kate Kenny

'Cruel optimism' names a relation of attachment to compromised conditions of possibility. What is cruel about these attachments, and not merely inconvenient or tragic, is that the subjects who have x in their lives might not well endure the loss of their object or scene of desire, even though its presence threatens their well-being, because whatever the content of the attachment, the continuity of the form of it provides something of the continuity of the subject's sense of what it means to keep on living on and to look forward to being in the world.

(Lauren Berlant, 2006)

How do workers experience the disintegrating structures and dissolving fantasies engendered by insecure employment, compulsory mobility and decline in living standards? What are the dynamics that keep fantasies of a good life alive even in the face of these changes? How can we apprehend the affective landscape of struggles for existence in the new world of work? Berlant's *Cruel Optimism* (2011) speaks directly to these questions. It details new ways in which we might understand the experiences of ordinary living for low-wage workers for whom life is one long series of crises that demand all of one's energy to negotiate. Merely staying afloat becomes a mammoth task, as the long-held fantasy of a better life fades away. Theories of affect and belonging, Berlant argues, can help us to approach such experiences.

While her ideas have not yet been drawn upon by organization scholars in any meaningful way, they hold significant potential for shedding light on some of the most important, albeit elusive, issues in the workplaces we study. This chapter sets out some of this potential. Lauren Berlant is professor of English at the University of Chicago, and her ideas are central to the study of what it is to be a citizen, with a particular focus on relations of intimacy and belonging.

She has long inspired scholars interested in the affective dynamics of attachments. Her work includes a trilogy on 'national sentimentality': *The Anatomy of National Fantasy* (1991), *The Queen of America Goes to Washington City* (1997) and *The Female Complaint* (2008), along with studies of intimacy, attachment and the public sphere including *Intimacy* (2000); *Our Monica, Ourselves: The Clinton Affair and the National Interest* (2001, with Lisa Duggan); *Compassion: The Culture and Politics of an Emotion* (2004) and *On the Case* (a special issue of *Critical Inquiry*, 2007). She blogs at www.supervalentthought.com and is also a founding member of the art/activist group Feel Tank Chicago. *Cruel Optimism* builds on these works in a unique attempt to depict existence in a world of ever-encroaching precarity. In the book, she focuses on the aesthetic, embodied and affective strategies of adjustment experienced by those at the forefront of drastic changes to work and welfare in contemporary United States and Europe.

In this chapter her ideas are illustrated through a recent account of a growing class of 'work-campers' in the United States in Jessica Bruder's *Nomadland* and its associated documentary. It paints a picture of life in the 'camperforce': an emerging group of retirement-age Americans who have unexpectedly encountered a decimation of wealth, and who now travel across the United States in old recreational vehicles, in search of minimum-wage and physically strenuous labour.

> In an era of disappearing pensions, wage stagnation, and widespread foreclosures, Americans are working longer and leaning more heavily than ever on Social Security, a program designed to supplement (rather than fully fund) retirement. For many, surviving the golden years now requires creative lifestyle adjustments. And for those riding the economy's outermost edge, adaptation may now mean giving up what full-time RV dwellers call 'stick houses' to hit the road and seek work.
>
> (Bruder, 2014)

This account powerfully depicts life amid the 'first-ever reversal in retirement security in modern U.S. history', according to Monique Morrissey of the Economic Policy Institute in Washington, D.C.

Cruel optimism

Cruel optimism is Berlant's term for describing situations in which a thing we desire – it could be food, a relationship, a fantasy of a certain kind of life or a political ideology – stands in the way of our flourishing.

The relationship is optimistic and turns cruel when the attachment itself is what actively prevents us from achieving the aim that attracted us to it in the first place. The book of the same name illustrates these ideas with reference to attachments to a variety of scenes ranging from romantic love, the improvement of one's social status and the pursuit of political utopias. What connects all of these, and structures her argument overall, is the fantasy of the 'good life', which at once encompasses moral, intimate and economic spheres of experience. Bruder's *Camperforce*, for example, is replete with attachments to scenes of a better life in retirement, attainable through work.

Berlant queries the persistence of certain scenes of desire within this fantasy: reciprocal and fulfilling relations with loved ones, political systems that care for all, equitable workplaces, upward mobility and space for enjoyment and pleasure within this. How do they survive while evidence of their very precarity and instability is all around us? What makes these dreams seem possible and worthy of effort, even in the face of clear evidence to the contrary? Here enters fantasy, which sutures contradictory elements to create an overall sense of existential coherence. The question for Berlant is what happens when these fantasies begin to fall apart; what repairs the suture and keeps things in place? Her work explores this against a backdrop of the continued retreat of social democratic projects in post–World War II Western nations, as states withdraw involvement in for example the redistribution of wealth and invite ever-increasing inequality. Her specific focus is on post-1980s United States and Europe.

In her national sentimentality trilogy, Berlant developed these themes through examining the development of aesthetic, erotic and political expression in the United States over a period of 200 years. Her focus then was on the affective dynamics underscoring both citizenship but also engagement in the public sphere. With a clear development of these ideas, *Cruel Optimism* extends the reach of the affective dynamics that she had argued drove a sense of belonging to a nation and a polity. It attempts to bring these ideas to bear on the now; it is contemporary experiences of the social that she is interested in. It also moves beyond the United States to examine contemporary Europe.

Her way of working is to look at TV, film, newspapers and literature appearing since 1990 in order to 'seek out the historical sensorium that has developed belatedly since the fantasmatic part of the optimism about structural transformation realized less and less traction in the world' (2011: 3). The focus here is on the 'ordinary' and how this becomes a continual, grinding scene of crisis that marks everyday life, so much so that such scenes cease to feel like crises after a while.

The very labour of coping with these recurrent calamities becomes all-encompassing in itself, leaving little time for anything else including those activities seen as necessary for 'flourishing'. Some key concepts contribute to the development of her overall arguments.

Time and ordinariness

Berlant deals with time and the experience of it in an innovative and exciting way. She is focused on the mundane. Rather than simply an empirical noticing, she is interested in the very construction of the ordinary; the flows and energies that mark existence in the everyday and how these emerge and are shaped by new social structures instituted by contemporary forms of capitalism.

It is the existence of those at the bottom of such structures with which she is most concerned. A scene of 'crisis ordinariness' marks a state of being under such conditions; day-to-day efforts to merely stay afloat take over. All the while, corporate-sponsored dreams and desires to attain the 'good life' persist in a cruel and unattainable manner, even as people 'scramble for modes of living on' (2011: 8).

Unpacking these temporal dynamics, Berlant tries to understand how it is that things that hurt us including flawed fantasies of a better life become embedded, and *ordinary* over time, so that hurtful connections become a part of existence. There is a perverse enjoyment in their very regularity: 'one of optimism's ordinary pressures is to induce conventionality, that place where appetites find a shape in the predictable comforts of the good-life genres that a person or a world has seen fit to formulate' (2011: 2). In other words, the pleasure in the attachment comes from the way it slips into our day-to-day life: how it sits within the predictable comforts therein.

> 'The first time you sleep in your car downtown, you feel like a horrible failure or a homeless person,' said Silvianne Delmars, who worked stowing merchandise at the Fernley warehouse. 'But that's the great thing about people: we make everything habit.' Delmars was a tarot reader who had suffered a run of bad luck: a stolen car, a broken wrist (no insurance), a house in New Mexico that she couldn't sell.

In Silvianne's account we see a juxtaposition of ideals of the good life in which success is represented by a stable home, and the ordinariness of crisis in which this ideal has fallen apart. For Berlant the challenge is how to apprehend this present. Once it takes place, the present moment quickly becomes translated into something else, something comprehensible. But contemporary moments arrive at us in an affective manner; 'the present is what makes itself present to us before it becomes anything else', including say an event, or even an era that we can reflect back upon. The present is therefore an affect, albeit one that is mediated by other forces including the way in which situations are filtered both personally and in public. In scenes of crisis ordinariness then, the question is how narratives of the present can be managed and made sense of even where many emerge at once, and that frequently contradict each other. Some present themselves as possible, while others are blocked.

In her understanding of such scenes, Berlant develops the idea of the impasse. This is a period of time in which one becomes acutely aware of the immanence of the world, its complexity and its demands, because of an accelerated sense of crisis. Life in the impasse demands an unceasing vigilance, a 'wandering absorptive awareness' (2011: 4) in which one must remain alert, actively gathering any information that might help make sense of the new and rapidly shifting context into which one has been thrown. There is no rest; the struggle for stability is what marks existence here.

> At sixty, (May) the silver-haired grandmother lacked electricity and running water. She couldn't find work. Her unemployment benefits had run out, and her daughter's family, with whom she had lived for many years while holding a series of low-wage jobs, had recently downsized to a smaller apartment. There wasn't enough room to move back in with them.

For Berlant, the impasse refers to a temporal period in which existence becomes stuck; moving forward is not yet possible. Situations of impasse can emerge and be experienced differentially depending on the various gender, class, racial and other structural intersections at which the subject finds herself, a point for which she draws upon Ranciere (2011: 5).

Breaking from existing understandings of the subject under contemporary neoliberalism, Berlant treats us to an alternative way of apprehending a life lived among 'crisis ordinariness', this slow beat of survival amid constant change and uncertainty, where as she notes 'adjustment' itself 'seems like an accomplishment'. Simply treading water to stay afloat takes all of one's energy and mean that all people can do is watch the fading fantasy of the good life move ever further away. Again we see this with Bruder's description of Linda May:

> ... A couple of years later, May found herself close to the edge again. She was working as a Home Depot cashier for $10.50 an

hour, which barely paid for her $600-a-month trailer in Lake Elsinore, California. She wondered, not for the first time, how anybody could afford to grow old. She had held many jobs in her life — building inspector, general contractor, flooring-store owner, insurance executive, cocktail waitress — but none had brought even a modicum of lasting financial security. 'Never managed to get myself a pension,' said May, who wears bifocals with rose-colored plastic frames and reveals deep laugh lines when she smiles, which is often. She knew she would soon be eligible for Social Security benefits, but at $499 her monthly checks would not even cover the rent.

For Berlant, this present that comprises a time of 'stretched-out' crisis marks a radical break. It evokes a new kind of temporality that stands in contrast to our previous experiences of upheaval and rapid change. Now the exceptional happening is no longer exceptional; crisis becomes ordinary while survival amid such scenes is a qualitatively different battle. New theories and approaches are needed, because the existing perspectives, including for example trauma theory, no longer apply. What is being experienced is more than the temporally truncated shocks that lead to trauma, but a drawn out and mundane sense of panic.

In addition to Bruder's account of retirement age and migrant workers in precarious jobs, Berlant's focus on the ordinary everyday chimes with recent work within organization studies that draws on affect theory (Harding and Lee, 2014; Kenny and Fotaki, 2014). The idea is that an attentiveness to affect enables us to appreciate and also to represent the texture of day-to-day experience: the quality of embodied existence (Sedgwick, 2003). The researcher is deeply implicated in these flows and rhythms, staying open to their impacts rather than adopting a detached, neutral stance (McCormack, 2008). The question of how to do this remains challenging; new and innovative 'methods' are needed (Fotaki et al., 2016). Organization scholars have explored various ways in which this might be done as exemplified in a recent special issue on the topic. Ashcraft (2016), for example, describes the ordinary affects implicated in day-to-day experiences of academic labour under recent neoliberal management structures within universities. Michels and Steyaert (2016) examines such momentary scenes with a study of emergent performances on the part of working musicians in Berlin's public spaces, while Pullen et al. (2016) explore the everyday as a process of open-ended becoming during which the subject is always in connection albeit that this is rarely acknowledged in theories that aim to explain working life. This, they argue, opens up an exploration of the 'radical potential in the everyday' by querying what bodies can do, and how they relate to the ambivalent affects generated by the organizations we work for. The challenge is to develop such new approaches in order to really engage with the 'sticky pragmatics of right now, right here' (Seigworth and Gregg, 2010:14). To such debates, Berlant shows how the historical present is encountered affectively before it is understood in other ways, and she highlights the struggles to adjust against backdrops of precarious, contingent conditions of work and life.

Cruel attachments

To help us understand this temporal persistence of flawed attachments, Berlant describes the nature of the attachment itself. It is affectively structured so that we retain a recurring inclination to keep returning to 'the scene of the fantasy', on each occasion hoping and indeed expecting that this time our being close to it will help our world to change in the way we want it. The object of desire is, she argues, neither a thing nor a relation but rather is best understood as a 'cluster of promises magnetized by a thing that appears as an object but is really a scene in the psychoanalytic sense' (2011: 16). The scene inspires and evokes a world of possibility that opens up each time we return to it.

> May began fantasizing about her next destination, which would be warmer and less exhausting. Like many of her neighbors, she planned a pilgrimage to Quartzsite, Arizona, a migrants' Shangri-la in the Sonoran Desert. The full-time residents of the town number only about 3,400. But every year, several hundred thousand RV dwellers gather there to spend the winter parked amid towering saguaro cacti. Many take advantage of the federal public land, where they're allowed to 'boondock' without the usual utility hookups for free, powering their rigs with solar panels or gas generators. They go financially dormant, spending almost no money. One workamper described Quartzsite as 'Burning Man for geezers'. And not surprisingly, corporate recruiters follow the migration there.

Berlant's account evokes and to some degree echoes ideas on attachments to flawed but damaging 'scenes' as described by others, from Butler's 'passionate attachments' to normative and hurtful discourses of gender and sexuality (2004) for which she draws upon Lacan's ideas, to Wendy Brown's work on Foucauldian dynamics of subjection in which politically marginalized and injured groups actively invest in their marginalization because the persistent memory of suffering remains constitutive of one's very identity (1995). Berlant sets her position apart from these. While a melancholic condition that underscores for example Butler's account of a painful attachment describes how the subject holds on to a past experience of loss as this becomes 'internalized' in the constitution of one's ego, cruel optimism is about future losses. It describes retaining attachment to a scene that promises to cause one future pain, prior to this loss. Thus it describes an optimistic desire for a malevolent set of promises.

Scholars working with post-Foucauldian approaches to subjectivity, particularly Butler's concept of passionate attachment to power – the idea that we subject ourselves to normative discourses in order to be able to persist as liveable beings – will find particular interest in Berlant's discussion, critique and alternatives to this problem, and the alternative model of infantile dependency outlined in the fifth chapter of *Cruel Optimism*.

What is cruel about this optimism: what harshness underscores it? There are two ways in which the relation is cruel; first where the object itself is what renders the transformation that is required and desired impossible; the change is hampered by the very presence of the problematic thing.

> They also demand little in the way of benefits or protections. On the contrary, ... most expressed appreciation for whatever semblance of stability their short-term jobs offered. Take fifty-seven-year-old Joanne Johnson, who was dashing upstairs last October at Amazon's Campbellsville facility when she tripped and fell, striking her head on a conveyor-belt support bar. She was bandaged up at AmCare — an in-house medical station — and then rushed to an emergency room. The episode left her with two black eyes and nine stitches along her hairline. 'They let me continue working. They didn't fire me,' Johnson recalled warmly. And the day after she was injured, a human-resources representative visited the RV she shared with her sixty-seven-year-old husband, a former workamper. Johnson, who had promised her employers that she would never run up the stairs again, was thunderstruck: 'We thought that was one of the most amazing things in the world, that he literally took time away to come to our door to see how we were doing.'

For this group of workers, a complex attachment to the situation stands in the way of demanding any meaningful change despite the hardships endured. Second, we become accustomed to the comforts of being in relation with the compelling cluster of hurtful promises. It sustains us and we are attached to the sustenance despite the problematic nature of its source. The danger emerges when 'a person or world finds itself bound to a situation of profound threat that is, at the same time, profoundly confirming' (2011: 2).

> Despite the boredom, May was grateful for one part of her job. 'The best thing was the camaraderie,' she said. 'I made friends there.' When she first reached the area around Fernley, hundreds of workampers were arriving on the same migratory wave and settling in as far as thirty-five miles from the Amazon warehouse.

Affective attachments to one's friends along with fantasies of a future 'good retirement' helped to sustain these scenes.

Cruel organizations

Contemporary workplaces are scenes in which fantasies of the good life are actively manufactured and reproduced. This was the case since the early 1900s during which industrialists including Henry Ford actively promoted a dream of personal advancement through consumption, enabled by hard work on the shop floor of his car factories. Since the 1980s in particular, the promise of upward mobility has increasingly been judged to be hollow as decreasing economic productivity and a rise in inequality yields an erosion of the traditional middle class and its traditional expectations of stability and generational advances in living standards.

> Of all the programs seeking workampers, the largest and most rapidly expanding is Amazon's CamperForce…Workampers are plug-and-play labor, the epitome of convenience for employers in search of seasonal staffing. They appear where and when they are needed. They bring their own homes, transforming trailer parks into ephemeral company towns that empty out once the jobs are gone. They aren't around long enough to unionize. On jobs that are physically difficult, many are too tired even to socialize after their shifts.

For Berlant the demise of the fantasy becomes clear in such contexts of the post-Fordist 'bad work' discussed in the films *Rosetta* and *La Promesse*, described in Chapter 5 of *Cruel Optimism*.

It is also clear in classic studies of contemporary working for example as Barbara Ehrenreich (2001) outlines in her journalistic account of 'treading water' to stay alive against the backdrop of the Welfare to Work scheme in 1990s United States. Here we see the 'bad work' at Walmart in which her sense of self is gradually eroded with drug tests, where survival becomes almost impossible as she tries to hold down enough jobs to meet her accommodation costs, but the simple struggle in doing this results in getting sick. In her low-paid and benefits-free employments, this is a luxury she simply cannot afford. 'Making ends meet' in such a world involves a series of equations that does not add up, she concludes. Ehrenreich describes how life during this time becomes about constantly trying to return to a brief reprieve of normality, a sense of rest that never comes.

Workplaces form the backdrop to the slow death of such dreams, in what Berlant refers to as the fraying of the fantasies. What sets her apart here is a continuous insistence that researchers' attention be trained at those surviving at the bottom of the social hierarchy created by contemporary capitalism. In management studies, in contrast, it often appears as though only the middle class/intelligentsia get to have complex attachments and affects (2011: 156), with those at the bottom of the hierarchy deemed to be simplistic dupes, either resisting or not.

This has certainly been the case in relation to organizational theorists. For sure, the idea that identities and subjectivities are multiple and complex has held sway in recent years, but empirical examinations of this have tended to draw on the professions only. We are over-loaded with studies of the vagaries of subject positions to which knowledge economy workers – consultants, accountants, media and creatives – are exposed. While scholars do examine low-paid work and precariat working, this tends to be carried out in a less nuanced, more sweeping manner. Studies of power and resistance for example proliferate from investigations into factory and call-centre working although this often yields a search for evidence of either 'resistance' or 'domination', echoing earlier studies such as Donald Roy's bananatime. A 'resistance/ domination' dualism is set up in relation to low-paid working: an 'either/ or' dichotomy. This binary leads to caricatures of those in lower-paid sectors that are not helpful.

Why is this the case? Berlant suggests that the aversion on the part of academics and scholars to approaching and trying to understand the precariat might in fact reflect what Ranciere, Philips and Agamben's describe as both fear and then hatred in relation to a sense of encroaching precarity on the part of those who were previously well-protected and who had been assured of this protection for the rest of their lives.

Precarity is coming for us all, but perhaps our peripheral consciousness of the threat engenders a repulsion for the topic and for those who represent it, alongside an aversion to knowing it in any depth beyond that which is necessary. In *Cruel Optimism*, Berlant illustrates this in relation to *Human Resources* and *Time Out* (2011: 195), films in which the incoming tide of precarity is encountered for the first time by resolutely middle-class employees.

Some authors point out that recognition of the precarity of others represents an opportunity for ethical engagement (Butler, 2009). The idea is that awareness of the precariousness of others makes us realize that we all 'live a life that is at risk from the outset', and which can be 'expunged quite suddenly from the outside and for reasons that are not always under one's control' (Butler, 2009: 30). No amount of personal wealth or influence can buffer us from our potential precariousness and our nearness to dying. This makes us acutely aware of our bodily vulnerability, in particular our dependency on others for survival through mutual support but also the formation and maintenance of institutions and social structures that facilitate shared assistance. Recognizing precarity as a 'generalizable condition' (2009: 23) evokes new ways of thinking and talking about personhood in which our interconnectedness informs a new 'ontology of the subject' that respects the humanity of the other and her entitlement to persist. For some, it heralds new approaches to business ethics (Fotaki, 2017; Fotaki and Prasad, 2015; Kenny and Fotaki, 2014).

Berlant, however, invites another understanding of our embodied and affective response to precarity. It could be that, afraid that our own foundations may soon be shattered, we as organization scholars experience a repulsion towards that which represents it, an unwillingness to know more, and an acute desire to 'pull up the ladder' behind us. Deliberate blindness under this view becomes part of ongoing knowledge production within academic disciplines, organization studies included. It is constitutive of the 'scriptural economy' that de Certeau describes when he talks about the middle class and their tools for maintaining the status quo. And this manifests itself in a theoretical and empirical 'blind spot' when it comes to low-paid work. In addition to offering an insight into why this blind spot exists, Berlant's *Cruel Optimism* opens up a new demand to extend understandings of scenes of complex attachment and struggle amid crises to all aspects of the work hierarchy, and particularly to those who experience upheavals, in its most raw and brutal form.

Overall, a richer picture that respects the subjectivity of those at the margins of working is required and for this reason Berlant's work represents exactly such an opportunity.

Apprehending cruelty and optimism

The inherent method in Berlant's admittedly 'anti-method' work can offer new insights into how to approach such an apprehension of scenes of crisis ordinariness in the context of workplaces. Her stance is one of 'ethical noticing': being in the present and remaining aware of small details as lives unfold, not least via a sensitivity to affect. This stands in contrast to other approaches to empirical data currently prevalent within the social sciences. Espeth Probyn (2010) describes how theorists of affect can often be among the more unfeeling of academics. She draws on Eve Sedgwick to point out that their work can be disengaged. In an evocative piece Probyn tells us that academics often only read in a way designed for gleaning ideas, while all the while thinking and focusing on what they themselves are going to write. Academics' obsessions with collecting these nuggets helps us to ignore what else is there. Berlant's account of the pulsing refrains of affect that illuminate scenes of living amid crisis ordinariness prevents such an orientation.

Ideas of 'self-abeyance' and 'lateral drifting' open up an account of how people exist in the impasse of life at the bottom, in ways that cannot be reduced to simple resistance or intentionality – there is no 'call to consciousness' there, an insight rich in its potential for organizational scholars and social theorists more generally. As Lefebvre argues, affect infuses working life but in unusual ways – life is not about the active carrying out of one's job, but rather the brief moments, thoughts and encounters as one, for example, commutes to work: the flashes and shimmers that can occur. Together with Lawrence Grossberg (2010) and his 'mattering maps', in which he offers us a way of tracing such affects in music, Berlant's accounts of scenes help us to understand these shimmers. In this, her description of how we might do this resonates with Sedgwick's (2003) call for attention to the beat of intensities over the time of subjectivity, and Stewart's writing of affect into her description of 'bloom spaces'. It speaks to a small but growing group of organization scholars who continue to explore the potential of affect to shed light on 'the intensities and forces of organizational life' (Beyes and Steyaert, 2012: 52; see also Gabriel, 2014; Fotaki et al., 2016; Wood and Brown, 2011).

From Berlant, we learn for example how tightly people cling to 'a relation that invests an object/ scene with the promise of the world's continuity' (2011: 52), which helps us to understand the conservativism of those at the bottom, described in relation to films *Rosetta* and *La Promesse* (2011: 174–175), along with the wish to remain proximate to the fantasy of the good life, even as we know we will never possess it. The conception of a cluster of promises helps us to see the incoherence and complexity of negotiation, bargaining and 'the survival strategies we attach to affects' (2011: 49).

From the perspective of (anti-) method, *Cruel Optimism* represents an unusual move away from the subject under study and towards the others that surround her. The book is laced with instances of scenes of dealing with loved ones' own attachments, affective bargains with sites of promise of relationality to come and proximate identifications. Within this, the 'messy dynamics of attachment, self-continuity, and the reproduction of life that are the material scenes of living in the present' emerge and Berlant shows the role affectivity plays in illuminating this. Here, subjects' negotiations and bargains with their proximate others (as depicted in, for example, the relationship of child to parent) is generally left out of organization theory. The 'others' of those we study begin and end with their colleagues, and even this extension is rare. Ehrenreich's account of life at the bottom is a singular one (some exceptions include Walkerdine's accounts of pit closures in Wales (2010) and Gregg's (2010) discussion of office friendships).

What does this all mean for the study of work? It amounts to another level of work, because it evokes the work involved in just staying still, in maintaining your place in the world; it is a kind of 'work upon work'. Given the complexity of others' attachments that colour it, and the requirement to work on their promises too, perhaps it represents a state of 'work upon work, upon work'. Moreover, this work upon work amounts to neither 'domination' with a big D nor resistance with a big 'R', but mere ongoingness, survival and mundane existence. In this layering, Berlant enriches how we might approach the subjective experience of work today, not least for ethnographies of workplaces.

Within this then, the question of affect and its relation to emotion is key. Throughout the text, Berlant reminds us that emotions cannot be trusted: 'often emotions vary while the affective structure remains', she points out, elsewhere noting that 'an optimistic attachment is invested in one's own or the world's continuity, but might *feel* any number of ways, from the romantic to the fatalistic, to the numb to the nothing (2011: 13), or my personal favourite: 'All babies smile, but it may be gas'. Thus she echoes the ambivalence of affect scholars in relation to emotion, with many arguing that while the two concepts are often used interchangeably, clear distinctions are needed (Fotaki et al., 2016). For Deleuze (2005) and Massumi (2002) for example, invoking emotions necessitates an unhelpful process of categorization as complex feelings are typologized into one emotional state or another, which stands against our being able to experience the rich texture of the world as it is experienced. An overall suspicion of emotion characterizes her work. In place, Berlant offers us an account of intuition as a means to understand desire and fantasy as they play out in life in the impasse: she describes subjects in question as 'a historically capacious, neo intuitive sense of becoming-present'. Contemporary transformative forces compel us to adopt, not stabilizations of being nor profoundly dissociated states, but instead 'sensually porous intuitive quandaries that stand in for the drive not to repeat the past in the making of contemporary history'. Intuition is subtle however and it is quiet. This echoes Sedgwick's work on desire and its quiet, temporal patterns, the subtleties of desire as it moves across the life of the subject (2014).

With all this talk of quiet intuition in place of emotion, how can we know that the 'repairs' described by Sedgwick, or indeed any of Berlant's desire-driven scenes, are taking place? As she notes,

> those of us who think for a living are too well-positioned to characterize certain virtuous acts of thought as dramatically powerful and right, whether effective or futile; we are set up to overestimate the proper clarity and destiny of an idea's effects and appropriate affects.
>
> (2011: 124)

To echo this in relation to affect she argues that subjects don't even know of their own affective attachments, they are always chasing after them, urging them to 'wait up!' Given this, Berlant appears to suggest that it is in writing styles like Sedgwick's description of grace and sense, or Stewart's bloom spaces, in which our best chances to affectively evoke life in the impasse lie. They are also present in the kinds of video and textual accounts of contemporary encounters with life in the impasse, described by Bruder.

> She played mind games to carve up the hours. 'I'm only staying here five more minutes, then I'm leaving. I'm quitting. This is it!' she told herself over and over. Then, a couple of hours before sunrise, she and her fellow workers would clock out and queue up to pass through a bank of metal detectors installed as part of the company's antitheft strategy.
>
> Meanwhile, the winter didn't let go so easily. There were mandatory fifty-hour overtime weeks. And May had a health scare... two weeks before her last day at the warehouse in Fernley, she began having dizzy spells... At the hospital in Reno, half an hour's drive west, May underwent a CAT scan and an X-ray but received no conclusive diagnosis. 'The nurse at the hospital said I could have compressed something on the vagus nerve,' May recalled. 'That'll make you pass out. You can get it from straining.' She sounded skeptical, since she didn't think she had been pushing

herself that hard. In any case, she was instructed to follow up with her primary-care physician. ('Yeah, I'd do that if I had one,' she said, laughing. Like most workampers I met, May was uninsured.) She paid $172 for a cab back to Sage Valley RV Park. For the next few days, she felt weak, took time off.

Later, in Quartzsite, I asked May how she'd felt finishing work on December 30. She didn't hesitate. 'Let me get the hell out of here!' she remembered thinking. 'Put the pedal to the metal. Let's go!'

Conclusion

Cruel Optimism offers valuable insights into workers' experiences of scenes in which taken for granted structures fall apart and suggests nuanced ways for approaching the study of these dynamics. There are aspects of her theory that might be expanded further; for example, while Berlant argues that the trajectory of her work is now 'transnational', in the context of *Cruel Optimism*, this amounts to adding contemporary Europe to a raft of U.S. examples. Questions emerge as to what this would look like in other contexts, for example in the countries that have long played host to the offshoring of the more repressive forms of low-paid, insecure work contracts as these are deemed unsuitable for labour markets in the more expensive 'West'. What scenes of crisis ordinariness emerge here, what are the complexities within and what are the felt responses? These questions prompt further research into this valuable new approach for organization studies.

Recommended reading

Original text by Lauren Berlant

Berlant, L. (2011) *Cruel Optimism*. Durham, NC: Duke University Press.

Key academic text

Cooley, W. (2013) Cruel Optimism by Lauren Berlant (Review). *American Studies* 52(3): 79–80. Project MUSE. doi:10.1353/ams.2013.0065

Accessible resource

McCabe, E. (2001) Depressive Realism: An Interview with Lauren Berlant. In *Hypocrite Reader*, Vol. 5. Available: http://hypocritereader.com/5/depressive-realism. Accessed 8 February 2018.
Bruder, J. Camperforce. Documentary. Available: https://harpers.org/blog/2017/12/camperforce/

References

Ashcraft, K. L. (2016) "Submission" to the Rule of Excellence: Ordinary Affect and Precarious Resistance in the Labour of Organization and Management Studies. *Organization* 24(1): 36–58.

Berlant, L. (1991) *The Anatomy of National Fantasy.* Chicago, IL: University of Chicago Press.

Berlant, L. (1997) *The Queen of America Goes to Washington City.* Durham, NC: Duke University Press.

Berlant, L. (2006) 'Cruel Optimism', Differences. *A Journal of Feminist Cultural Studies* 17(5): 21.

Berlant, L. (2008) *The Female Complaint.* Durham, NC: Duke University Press.

Berlant, L. (2011) *Cruel Optimism.* Durham, NC: Duke University Press.

Berlant, L., 2014. *Compassion: The culture and politics of an emotion.* New: Routledge.

Beyes, T., and Steyaert, C. (2012) Spacing Organization: Non-Representational Theory and Performing Organizational Space. *Organization* 19: 45–61.

Brown, W. (1995) *States of Injury: Power and Freedom in Late Modernity.* Princeton, NJ: Princeton University Press.

Bruder, J. (2014) The End of Retirement: When You Can't Afford to Stop Working. *Harpers*, August. Available: https://harpers.org/archive/2014/08/the-end-of-retirement/?single=1 Accessed 8th February 2018.

Butler, J. (1997) *The Psychic Life of Power: Theories in Subjection.* London: Routledge.

Butler, J. (2009) *Frames of War.* New York: Verso.

Deleuze, G. (2005) *Francis Bacon: The Logic of Sensation* (D. W. Smith, Trans.). Minneapolis: University of Minnesota Press.

Ehrenreich, B. (2001) *Nickel and Dimed: On (Not) Getting By in America.* New York: Metropolitan Books.

Fotaki, M. (2017) Relational Ties of Love – A Psychosocial Proposal for Ethics of Compassionate Care in Health and Public Services. *Psychodynamic Practice* 27(2): 181–189.

Fotaki, M., Kenny, K., and Vachhani, S. (2016) Thinking Critically About Affect in Organization Studies: Why It Matters. *Organization* 24(1): 3–17 [Editorial].

Fotaki, M. and Prasad, A. (2015) Questioning Neoliberal Capitalism and Economic Inequality in Business Schools. *Academy of Management Learning & Education* 14(4): 556–575.

Gabriel, Y. (2014) Disclosing Affect: A Freudian Inquiry into Organizational Storytelling. In K. Kenny and M. Fotaki (eds) *The Psychosocial and Organization Studies: Affect at Work*, pp. 83–103. Basingstoke: Palgrave Macmillan.

Gregg, M. (2010) On Friday Night Drinks: Workplace Affects in the Age of the Cubicle. In M. Gregg and G. J. Seigworth (eds) *The Affect Theory Reader*, pp. 250–268. London: Duke University Press.

Grossberg, L. (2010) Affect's Futurum: Rediscovering the Virtual in the Actual. In M. Gregg and G. Seigworth (eds), *The Affect Theory Reader*, pp. 309–338. London: Duke University Press.

Grosz, E. (2004) *The Nick of Time: Politics, Evolution and the Untimely*. Durham, NC: Duke University Press.

Harding, N. and Lee, H. (2014) The Doctor/Manager Relationship as a Psychosocial Encounter: A Scene of Fantasy and Domination? In K. Kenny and M. Fotaki (eds), *Affect at Work. Bringing the Psychosocial to Organizations and Organizing*, pp. 215–240. London: Palgrave.

Kenny, K. and Fotaki, M. (eds) (2014) *Affect at Work. Bringing the Psychosocial to Organizations and Organizing*. London: Palgrave.

Kenny, K. and Fotaki, M. (2015) From Gendered Organizations to Compassionate Borderspaces: Reading Corporeal Ethics with Bracha Ettinger. *Organization* 22(2): 183–199.

Massumi, B. (2002) *Parables for the Virtual: Movement, Affect, Sensation*. Durham, NC: Duke University Press.

McCormack, D. P. (2008) Thinking-spaces for Research Creation. *Inflexions* 1(1): 1–16.

Michels, C. and Steyaert, C. (2016) By Accident and by Design: Composing Affective Atmospheres in an Urban Art Intervention. *Organization* 24(1): 79–104.

Probyn, E. (2010) Writing Shame. In M. Gregg and G. Seigworth (eds), *The Affect Theory Reader*, pp. 71–92. Durham, NC: Duke University Press.

Pullen, A., Rhodes, C. and Thanem, T. (2016) Affective Politics in Gendered Organizations: Affirmative Notes on Becoming-Woman. *Organization* 24(1), 105–123.

Sedgwick, E. K. (2003) *Touching Feeling: Affect, Pedagogy, Performativity*. Durham, NC: Duke University Press.

Seigworth, G. and Gregg, M. (2010). An Inventory of Shimmers. In M. Gregg and G. J. Seigworth (eds), *The Affect Theory Reader*, pp. 1–28. London: Duke University Press.

Stewart, K. (2010). Worlding Refrains. In M. Gregg and G. J. Seigworth (eds), *The Affect Theory Reader*, pp. 339–355. London: Duke University Press.

Walkerdine, V. (2010) Communal Beingness and Affect: An Exploration of Trauma in an Ex-Industrial Community. *Body and Society* 16(1): 91–116.

Wood, M. and Brown, S. (2011) Lines of Flight: Everyday Resistance along England's Backbone. *Organization* 18(4): 517–539.

6   Judith Butler

Theorist and political activist

Nancy Harding

Judith Butler, a hugely influential but also controversial theorist, is a philosopher whose writings are not often found on the bookshelves labelled 'philosophy'. Her job title is 'Professor of Comparative Literature', but her work on literature is a very small part of her oeuvre. An avowed feminist, her early, major books *Gender Trouble* and *Bodies that Matter* are seminal within queer theory.[1] What is in no doubt is that she is one of the most important theorists in feminist and gender studies and her influence extends across disciplines, contributing not only to feminist, gender or queer accounts in those disciplines, but to new ways of thinking through and theorizing some major issues for academia in the 21st century. These include, for example, what form of left-wing politics might emerge to combat the rise of far-right extremism; who can and cannot be classed as 'human' and therefore disposable or protected; and whose lives are made precarious by the actions of governments?

Butler's work has provoked significant interest in management and organization studies, both through its influence on feminist or gender theories of work but also because her thesis of performativity (whose meaning will be unfolded in the next section) offers ways of understanding management, organizations and work more generally. Sometimes inadequate attention has been paid to the nuances of this influential theory, perhaps not surprisingly because her earlier works in particular are very difficult to absorb even after several readings. It could be tempting, after struggling with her early work, to ignore her later publications. This would be wrong because her account of performativity has developed. This chapter tracks those changes, showing how an increasingly sophisticated but more accessible account of performativity has evolved in her writing. Butler's more recent work focused on developing a new radical politics through a feminist ethics of precarity and relationality and continues to build on her account of performativity. This chapter barely touches the surface of Butler's influence in management and organization studies to date due to space constraints; rather it will look to the future and how, through tracking Butler's evolving thought, possibilities for a new politics of working lives may be developed.

Judith Butler: performativity (or not performativity)

I first encountered Butler's work when I pulled a book from the 'new in' shelves in the bookshop at the University of Leeds (UK) in 1997. I opened it and read:

> As a form of power, subjection is paradoxical. To be dominated by a power external to oneself is a familiar and agonizing form power takes. To find, however, that what 'one' is, one's very formation as a subject, is in some sense dependent upon that very power is quite another.
>
> (Butler, 1997a, pp. 1–2)

I read on, baffled but intrigued. This was a mind-expanding encounter – wow! But frustration: I couldn't understand what it meant although I knew that it could have consequences about how to think, talk and speak, how to analyze the workplace, and perhaps how to be human. I bought the book, read it in the quiet interludes at a conference, made copious notes, but still could not comprehend Butler's complexity. Defeated, I put it away but tried reading it again one Christmas and some glimmer of understanding developed. It was only on my fifth reading, a few years later and after I'd similarly struggled with her first two books, *Gender Trouble* (1990) and *Bodies that Matter* (1993), that the first book (1997a) made sense. My 'aha' moment was when I realized that each chapter in *Psychic Life of Power* tracks a stage in Hegel's account of the birth of self-consciousness. Each of these stages is re-interpreted through Freud, Althusser, Foucault and others. The result is a theory of the moment-to-moment emergence of the self within and through power; it is (in my interpretation at least) an expanded insight into Butler's theory of performativity, a peak into the complex micro-drama that takes place in each performative moment.

I am starting this chapter with this personal account because Butler is a philosopher who does not sit at her stove, *a la* Descartes, looking out at and pondering about 'the world', but is actively and very politically involved in it. Her difficult language belies what we could call a philosophy of the streets: this is life as it is lived, seen through the lens of someone trying to understand how it comes to be lived in such ways, with what effects, and how resistance can be articulated. Each encounter with her work is therefore not an exercise in understanding seemingly arcane and abstract ideas: it is a call to (non-violent) arms. Her work on performativity calls us to some form of political action, even if it is no more than learning to be kinder to ourselves through understanding how the norms that both subject and subjectify us require us to aspire to become that which we cannot.

Latterly, since perhaps *Frames of War* (2009a), Butler's political intent is more explicit. She is developing a left-wing politics that emerges out of her theory of performativity and is located firmly within her new focus on precarity. However, Butler has always been politically active: the very act of developing theory, she argues, is a form of political practice. That is

> theory is itself transformative, although it is not sufficient for social and political transformation. Something besides theory must take place, such as interventions at social and political levels that involve actions, sustained labor, and institutionalized practice .... [I]n all of these practices, theory is presupposed.
>
> (Butler, 2004b, p. 204)

My aim now is to track how Butler has developed her theory of performativity since *Gender Trouble* (1990). I will devote little attention to the still-developing theory of precarity because of the relevance of the former theory to 'critical performativity', a theory of political practice developing in critical management studies that draws, somewhat loosely, on Butler's theory of performativity. Tracking the increasing sophistication of Butler's analysis allows me to suggest that if 'critical performativity' is to become a form of political practice, it needs a far more nuanced understanding of 'performativity', one that builds on the potential for political action that already exists within Butler's work.

I am not, save for a few references, tracking how Butler's work has been used by management scholars. This is purely for reasons of space. There are some inspirational Butlerian interpreters within our discipline, including Kate Kenny (2010), Kat Riach, Melissa Tyler and Nick Rumens (2014, 2016) and others (see, for example, Hancock and Tyler, 2007), to name but a few. My focus is on deeper understanding of how Butler's theory of performativity has evolved so as to inform robust new theoretical insights and practical recommendations for a politics of organization studies.

Performativity

Butler's influence starts, famously, with her interrogation of how sex and gender are performatively constituted. Where feminist constructionists had argued that the female learns how to become female through conforming with the rules, norms, descriptors and so on of her biological sex, Butler (1990, 1993) argued that biology itself is constituted – there is nothing in 'nature' that determines there will be two (or more) sexes. In the preface to her book *Gender Trouble* (1990, p. viii), Butler asks:

> What configuration of power constructs the subject and the Other, that binary relation between 'men' and 'women' and the internal stability of those terms?

Her task in *Gender Trouble* (1990) and its successor, *Bodies that Matter* (1993), is to bring into question the epistemic/ontological regimes of sex and gender. Note, for example, how in the above quote the categories of 'men' and 'women' are destabilized by being put in quotation marks. Those small marks encapsulate the argument that

> Gender ought not to be conceived merely as the cultural inscription of meaning on a pregiven sex ...; gender must also designate the very apparatus of production whereby the sexes themselves are established.
> (1990, p. 6)

In that same chapter Butler also explains heterosexuality as a binary regime that '*requires* a stable and oppositional heterosexuality' (1990, p. 22, emphasis added), but that also *produces* masculine and feminine. This introductory chapter developed both a radical new feminist theory and developed seminal arguments in queer theory.

How then do these binary pairs, 'the man' and 'the woman', emerge, if the sexes are not natural, biological and pre-given? Butler's argument, famously, is that sex is performatively constituted:

> gender proves to be performative – that is, constituting the identity it is purported to be. In this sense, gender is always a doing, though not a doing by a subject who might be said to pre-exist the deed.
> (1990, pp. 24/25)

Butler's influence is J.L. Austin's (1962) *How to Do Things with Words* that had introduced the neologism 'performative' utterance. Austin argued that some, but not all, speech acts are 'performative', that is, by saying something they do something. However, Austin presumed that the subject who speaks precedes the words that are spoken; that is, the judge who announces 'I sentence you to imprisonment' is a judge who speaks, and in so speaking performs the act of imprisonment. Butler reversed this, suggesting that 'the subject who speaks is also constituted by the language that she or he speaks, [so] language is the condition of possibility for the speaking subject, and not merely its instrument of expression' (Butler, 1997a: 28). The judge, in this view, emerges as a judge because of her formation within and through discourses of law, and pronouncing a sentence of imprisonment constitutes the speaker as 'judge'. That is:

> Where there is an 'I' who utters or speaks and thereby produces an effect in discourse, there is first a discourse which precedes and enables that 'I' ...... Thus there is no 'I' who stands behind discourse and executes its volition or will through discourse.
>
> (Butler, 1993, p. 242)

It follows that:

> One is subjected [forced to conform] and subjectified [become a subject that has subjectivity] within discourses, and becomes a subject through performativity, which is not an act, nor a performance, but constantly repeated 'acts' that reiterate norms.
>
> (Butler, 1993, p. 12; 240 ff.)

Note the importance of 'constantly repeated acts' – these are fundamental to performativity. A 'repeated stylization of the body' is achieved through a myriad of acts that are undertaken within 'a highly rigid regulatory frame'. These acts 'congeal over time to produce the appearance of substance, of a natural sort of being' (1990, p. 33). Hence, rather than being born gendered, or become socialized into gender, we emerge as male or female through performatively constituting the identity of 'woman' or 'man'. Constantly repeated micro-movements of bodies, consisting of tiny acts, repeated over and over, occur within a set of meanings that influence each of these tiny, repeated acts. These meanings pre-exist us: born into them we learn how to move within them to 'constitute the illusion of an abiding gendered self' (1990, p. 140). The power of this statement struck me some while ago when I was sitting on a bench at Leeds' main railway station during the morning rush hour, facing the hordes of people who flowed off the trains, through the concourse, around the bench on which I sat, and out to the city centre. Nearly every one of those myriad of persons could be easily categorized as 'male' or 'female': their hair; their clothes, the ways in which they moved their bodies; the accoutrements they carried with them and how they used their bodies to carry them, each marked them as on one side or other of the binary. Each step could be one of those moment-to-moment constitutive movements. That is, walking is not merely perambulation: the differences between how bodies were moved in the process of putting one foot in front of the other, how clothes hung around those bodies and moved or did not move with them, how hair framed the face and how bags were carried were all 'dictated' by the norms of gender *and* in being enacted as a (suddenly very complex) step was a performative act that, being repeated over and over, performatively constituted an actor as recognizably 'female' or 'male'.[2]

That is how I then interpreted Butlerian notions of performativity. There will be other interpretations – the difficulty of her prose assures us of this.

A brief diversion: Butler in management and organization studies

There are numerous references to Butler's work in management and organization studies (MOS), but many use her work just as one reference amongst many, ignoring its theoretical insights. Those who support Borgerson's (2005) passionate advocacy of the value of Butler's work for MOS have brought very interesting insights into the discipline. The majority, perhaps unsurprisingly, aim to develop understanding of the performative constitution of gendered identities at the workplace.

An exemplary paper by Tyler and Cohen's (2010) provides an analysis of organizational 'spaces that matter', that is, spaces imbued with power relations that materialize gender. This empirical study investigates the use, by women, of office space and artefacts that constitute a gendered identity in conformity with organizational gender norms. Through this work, we see the 'normal' woman who is 'acceptable in organizational terms' (p. 192), that is, she is someone who is materialized within the narrow confines of the heteronormative matrix. Their work is a challenge to the continuing predilection of organization theorists to essentialize gender through seeking avidly to study (apparent) differences between sharply distinguished 'men' and 'women'. Rittenhofer and Gatrell's (2012) powerful Butlerian critique of such research argues that such unquestioned and unexamined assumptions about gender constitute the norms within which gender is performatively constituted. That is, by saying that, for example, women leaders are more people-focused, compassionate and caring than male leaders, women learn they *must* be people-focused, compassionate and caring, and men that they should be the opposite. Rittenhofer and Gatrell (2012) counter such approaches with a Butlerian challenge to dominant notions of gender. They oppose the fixity of essentialized gender with instability, and critique other dominant, essentialist concepts such as trait theories, teleology and homogeneity.

Extending the analysis from gender to other domains, the power of Butlerian thinking can be seen in Parker's (2001) seminal advocacy of queer theory for MOS. He identifies the potential in Butler's work for 'queering theory itself' (p. 37), that is, disrupting the power of the academy to constitute organizational 'reality' through the theories it develops. Such 'working at the site of ontology' of business schools (Ozturk and Rumens, 2014, p. 513) could take forward existing critiques of the work of business schools, going beyond arguing about the sustaining of neoliberalism and Western hegemony to challenge the foundations of that knowledge. Arguments that business school academics should engage more actively with businesses would come with a Butlerian warning about the extreme care needed to avoid non-felicitous performatives or constituting of 'realities' that are best avoided.

These paragraphs offer no more than brief indications of the ways in which Butlerian scholars in MOS are identifying the potential in Butler's philosophy for new insights about work and working lives.

Performativity expanded

It would be a mistake to assume that *Gender Trouble* (1990) and *Bodies that Matter* (1993) set out Butler's theory of performativity as if it were fully formed. She has continued to expand upon and develop the concept, formulating an ever-more insightful theory of how the social, psychic, historical, geographical, cultural, discursive, inter- and intra-subjective meet at and impinge upon performativity's accomplishments at the scene of the emergent and always-becoming 'I'. Butler often reminds readers of her earlier arguments, so that each book builds upon and extends her earlier work.

The Psychic Life of Power (1997a), as noted above, at least in my reading is an account of Hegel's theory of the coming of self-consciousness, each stage of which is encapsulated in each repeated, performative act. The focus here is on an extended understanding of Althusserian interpellation through locating it within and through the Hegelian scene of recognition and including a Freudian theory of attachment to subjection. This complex account argues that becoming a subject and thus having a liveable life requires that one is always within the social but also ek-static to the self, even as one absorbs and enacts requirements that incorporate pain and melancholy into the senses of the self. (At the risk of self-referentiality, I have discussed this at length, and applied it to management, in Chapter 2 of *On Being at Work: The Social Construction of the Employee* (Harding, 2013)).

The *Psychic Life of Power* was not the only book Butler published in 1997. The other, *Excitable Speech: A Politics of the Performative* (1997b), allows her to explore in great depth an issue that features throughout her work: a prior vulnerability to language. That is, (1997b, pp. 15/16)

> My presumption is that speech is always in some ways out of our control.... Untethering the speech act from the sovereign subject founds an alternative notion of agency and, ultimately, of responsibility .... The one who acts (who is not the same as the sovereign subject) acts precisely to the extent that he or she is constituted as an actor and, hence, operating within a linguistic field of enabling constraints from the outset.

Butler develops her arguments through an analysis of hate speech and makes a subtle and important contrast between injurious hate speech and the above-mentioned 'prior vulnerability to language' that arises from our being 'interpellated kinds of beings, dependent on the address of the other' (p. 26) for our very sense of a self. In my reading of *Excitable Speech* two things are of particular importance. First, speech is always-already injurious – we rely on it for our very being. But second, and importantly, we are not completely its puppets; we have agency. Language more generally cannot be protected against because we are subject to a *'primary dependency on a language we never made in order to acquire a tentative ontological status'*, but Butler emphasizes that one is not enslaved by language: speech can be disrupted and subverted and thus 'there is no mechanical and predictable reproduction of power' (p. 19). Hate speech can therefore be resisted or refused.

Gender Trouble (1990) and *Bodies that Matter* (1993) challenged ontologies of sex and gender. This, alongside her critique of Lacanian theory, is taken forward in *Antigone's Claim: Kinship between Life and Death* (2000) that undermines the ontology of kinship and the heterosexual family. Pragmatically, its critique of kinship is a challenge to the demand for 'gay marriage' on the grounds that such legal recognition of homosexual relationships would require conformity with heterosexual structures. Butler reads the Ancient Greek tragedy *The Antigone* to argue that there is no law that determines how kinship and the family should be understood – the nuclear family is not inevitable. In this book we see several (now familiar) Butlerian tropes at work, which together offer management scholars a method for critical analysis. First, as noted, there is the challenge to ontology(ies), here, again, the binary of woman and man alongside the concept of (Western) kinship. In the figure of Antigone, offspring of the incestuous relationship between Oedipus and Jocasta, Butler sees a woman who 'in some sense is also a man' (p. 61), because she takes the place of nearly every man in her family in the course of the drama, but at the same time she takes on many of the subject positions found in the heteronormative family even though she is outside the norms of that family. Second and relatedly, Butler again employs a Foucauldian argument in which she explores how something that is argued to be a law actively constitutes and creates that which it is ostensibly designed to prohibit. Thus, in this example, she argues that the incest taboo constitutes incest. Third (and I suggest this has become more important as her work has progressed) she questions the concept of the human, showing how some people are cast outside the identity of the human.

It is perhaps *Undoing Gender* (2004b) that illustrates most strongly how each of Butler's books builds on her earlier ideas, developing them and refining them, introducing new insights and polishing the older ones. Butler often summarizes her (evolving) theory in a very lucid language that suggests the value perhaps of reading her more recent summaries and then working backwards to *Gender Trouble* and *Bodies that Matter* so as to understand the formidable philosophy that informs her theory of performativity. In *Undoing Gender* (2004b) she writes (p. 212):

> the abiding assumption of my earlier gender theory was that gender is complexly produced through identificatory and performative practices, and that gender is not as clear or as univocal as we are sometimes led to believe. My effort was to combat forms of essentialism which claimed that gender is a truth that is somehow there, interior to the body, as a core or as an internal essence, something that we cannot deny, something which, natural or not, is treated as given.

Further (pp. 33/34):

> I have tried heretofore to argue that our very sense of personhood is linked to the desire for recognition, and that desire places us

outside ourselves, in a realm of social norms that we do not fully choose, but that provides the horizon and the resource for any sense of choice that we have. ..... Thus ... the discourse of rights avows our dependency, the mode of our being in the hands of others, a mode of being with and for others without which we cannot be.

This summarizes a continually evolving theory of the self: it has porous boundaries and is taken outside of itself. It exists beside itself, given over to others, in an ethical relation in a field of others in which its desire is for recognition and to become human. For some people, such recognition is foreclosed and they are denied entry to the category of the human. For them, their performative constitution of gender fails: they do not conform sufficiently with the norms that allow them to be recognizable as securely gendered and are outside the category of the human.

In *Undoing Gender* Butler's arguments still concern those whose gender or sexuality renders them fundamentally unintelligible, an impossibility, whose failure to conform with norms puts them outside the ranks of the human. Butler shifts her attention to the effects of American imperialism, exploring how the U.S. military can bomb entire populations it decides are outside the category of the human. However, in *Undoing Gender* Butler's focus remains upon gender, which, she argues, is a norm:

> Gender is a norm – a norm is not the same as a rule, and it is not the same as a law. A norm operates within social practices as the implicit standard of *normalization*. ... Norms ... usually remain implicit, difficult to read, discernible most clearly and dramatically in the effects that they produce. ... The question of what it is to be outside the norm poses a paradox for thinking, for if the norm renders the social field intelligible and normalizes that field for us, then being outside the norm is in some sense being defined still in relation to it. To be not quite masculine or not quite feminine is still to be understood exclusively in terms of one's relationship to the 'quite masculine' and the 'quite feminine'.
>
> (2004b, pp. 41/42)

Thus, she continues (p. 43), gender's insistence on the binary of man and woman is a 'regulatory operation of power' that forecloses the possibility of thinking differently. The norm is a form of social power that determines what is 'reality' and, importantly, produces 'the parameters of personhood'. But when someone who is non-normative, who is outside the field of the human, who is not fully categorizable or fully recognizable, insists on speaking and being heard, then in speaking beyond what is sayable they may shatter the consensus and evoke possibilities of resistance. To 'undo gender' is to move beyond the categories that define and enforce gender, to refuse to conform with norms (to undo them) and refuse to be securely gendered as female or male, or categorized by one's sexual desire. Such refusal is a political act that challenges the taken-for-granted, the 'law'.

But *Undoing Gender's* focus is not solely on gender; it is also on what constitutes 'the human' per se. For

> If we take the field of the human for granted, then we fail to think critically – and ethically – about the consequential ways that the human is being produced, reproduced, deproduced. …. The very notion of 'the human' is presupposed; it is defined in advance, and in terms that are distinctively western, very often American, and therefore parochial.
>
> (2004b, p. 221)

In this, Butler challenges the ontology of 'the human', suggesting that one becomes or fails to become human through performative constitutions of the self within scenes of power. This challenge opens the way for her turn to a theory of precarity in the short text *Precarious Life: The Power of Mourning and Violence* (2006) and the development of its arguments in *Frames of War: When Is Life Grievable* (2009a). Earlier, in *Giving an Account of Oneself* (2005), ethics and ethical action was interrogated by putting into question the subject that informs much ethical theory, from Ancient Greece to the present day. She argues that rather than there being a rational, self-aware subject who can learn how to be ethical, there are only people who are opaque to both themselves and others, never fully self-aware and not able to make the rational choices presupposed in utilitarian, deontological, virtue and other theories of ethics. Butler points to more productive ways of being an ethical individuating subject that is never separate and distinct from the social world in which it forms and is formed. These arguments are built on in *Senses of the Subject* (2015a), a collection of essays that is in some ways a rebuff to feminist new materialist critics who accuse her of ignoring materialities. *Senses of the Subject* builds on her previous work to account for the passions and the material within fields of power in which the subject is performatively constituted.

Precarious Life (2006), *Frames of War* (2009a), *Dispossession: The Performative in the Political* (2013, with Athena Athanasiou) and

Notes towards a Performative Theory of Assembly (2015b) mark a new, even more political turn in Butler's work, in which *precarity* emerges as her dominant theoretical focus. Her arguments start from an acknowledgement of the inherent vulnerability of human flesh. That is, 'anything living can be expunged at will or by accident' and it is the responsibility of social and political institutions to minimize conditions of precarity (2009b, p. ii). Either failure to do this, or framing certain populations so that they are seen as non-human, induces 'precarity', specifically 'that politically induced condition in which certain populations suffer from failing social and economic networks of support and become differentially exposed to injury, violence, and death' (ibid). Entire populations may suffer the conditions of precarity, or it may be individuals who are subjected to forms of violence for which the state offers little or no protection. Subjects not protected by the state or the law emerges through that neglect as differential effects of power. They come 'after' subjects because they do not count as subjects. Subjects may include individuals whose gender or sexuality are unrecognizable within contemporary normative regimes, and who thus 'embody the unthinkable and even the unlive-able' (p. iv). It is therefore the question of who does and does not count as a subject that links performativity and precarity, for the performative accomplishment of the 'I' requires recognition, and those who are not recognized, whose lives are not grievable, do not qualify as subjects (Butler, 2009b).

An illustration from my own work

Now that I have discussed how I have read Butler's theory of performativity as one that is evolving, I will explore the fruitfulness of the theory for MOS with an illustration from my own work that attempted to 'think with Butler's ideas'. Nearly every chapter in *Being at Work* (Harding, 2013) uses aspects of Butlerian theory to analyze one or two individuals' accounts of their work. My methodology was simple: for each chapter I chose an interview with one person, and I read and read the transcript of that interview to see which aspect of Butler's work might help me gain insights into that particular interviewee's account.

If it is possible to have a favourite chapter in one's own book, then it is Chapter 4, 'Being Human', in which I explore how an archaeologist, 'Alex', turns the very unglamorous job of digging in mud into the valorized identity of a professional. Butler's work alerts us to look for displacements, or contradictions in the stories people tell about themselves. There were three in Alex's: the job requires hard, dirty physical labour yet is a high status profession; she contrasted her student self's hatred of archaeological digs with her professional self's love of them; there were inexplicable differences between how she saw her work as an archaeologist and her work in an office. I used Butler's development of Althusser's theory of interpellation in *Psychic Life of Power* (1997a) and her reading of Sophocles' tragedy, *The Antigone*, in *Antigone's Claim* (2000) to think through Alex's account. The *Psychic Life of Power* explores how performativity is a social act requiring the recognition of others who say, in effect, 'yes, your actions lead me to acknowledge that this is who you are (or are not)'.

This analysis led me to realize that first, the identity of the other who grants recognition is vitally important in the performative constitution of the self – one does not turn to the interpellative hail of just anyone. Alex needed other archaeologists to confirm her own identity as a member of that profession: no-one else would suffice. Thus what is, objectively, the cold, wet and dirty labour of digging in the dirt becomes 'glamorous' when discussed with colleagues. Second, the act of talking about the profession as exciting and glamorous constitutes it as exciting and glamorous. Butler argues that language always-already precedes all speakers, as discussed above. Alex demonstrated to me how performativity requires that speakers carefully choose what words to use and which to reject from available discourses. Third, via *Antigone's Claim* Alex's account allowed me to explore the importance of friendship rather than the organization in granting recognition. Organizations can be oppressive: friends displace organizations, making them disappear, so to speak, and the self survives. Alex positioned the organization not so much as a controlling entity that required resistance for the self to exist, but as something of little importance. Rather than resistance there was insouciance. There is thus agency in performativity as Butler emphasizes.

Conclusion: implications for a more radical politics of work

For me, Butler's ideas make possible a far more insightful interrogation of empirical materials than formal methods of data analysis, but this requires grappling with her entire body of work and not just her two famous early books *Gender Trouble* and *Bodies that Matter* (see above). Her theory of performativity has developed in subtlety, comprehensiveness and philosophical power since then. One example illustrates this:

> gender performativity does not necessarily presuppose an always acting subject or an incessantly repeating body. It establishes a

complex convergence of social norms on the somatic psyche, and a process of repetition that is structured by a complicated interplay of obligation and desire, and a desire that is and is not one's own.

(2009b, p. xi)

I described above how, through watching people walking during the rush hour at Leeds train station, I thought I had understood Butler's theory of performativity. This quote shows how much I had still to learn. Were there space I could hazard an interpretation of the social norms converging on the somatic psyches of each of the people who passed me by, norms concerning needs engendered in neoliberal, capitalist cultures that invoke desires one thinks are one's own but that come at one, from outside, as it were.

The development of critical performativity as a new praxis within critical management studies locates its inspiration, albeit tenuously, within Butler's theory of performativity (see, for example, Spicer, Alvesson and Kärreman, 2009; Alvesson and Spicer, 2012; Wickert and Schaefer, 2015; Cabantous et al., 2016; Fleming and Banerjee, 2016; Learmonth et al., 2016; Spicer, Alvesson and Kärreman, 2016). Critical performativity is defined by its advocates as changing the language that managers speak so as to change management practices. Its critics (e.g. Cabantous et al., 2016) argue the theory is deeply flawed and based on a superficial understanding of Butler's work. If critical performativity is to achieve its aims of making meaningful change in the world of work, then it may benefit from deeper engagement with the work of this philosopher who is learning from her own experiences of treading the streets with protesters around the world.

Butler's work is not confined to understanding gender. It can and is used to interrogate 'organization', 'management' and any of the ontologies that govern our own discipline. For example, 'organizations' are established through apparatuses of production that have nothing to do with production lines, but through a host of other practices, norms, discourses and beliefs.

Further, it is important to note the continuing development of notions of resistance in Butler's work. This is especially so in her evolving theory of precarity, where mass assemblies are explored as a particular form of resistance. Resistance is a fault-line within critical management studies (Mumby, 2005). Butler may point us in the direction of new theories and practices of workplace resistance. For example, she emphasizes that it is not the individual who pre-exists acts of resistance: resistance becomes possible when norms, desires and discourses converge at the site of embodied personhood. Butlerian theory may provide insights for better understanding of a resistant form of political practice (see Harding, Ford and Lee, 2017). As noted above, for Butler theory *is* political practice, so perhaps we may find ways of developing theory that changes organizational norms.

Finally, for now, what potential is there within MOS for drawing on Butler's theory of precarity? Her focus is on populations suffering at the hands of Western, and specifically American imperialism, such as refugees, asylum seekers and the displaced, and those endangered by wars and violence. It may appear to demean those who suffer from such dehumanizing vectors to apply the theory to organizations, yet precarity undoubtedly describes the condition of people subjected to 'uberization' and other forms of insecure, temporary and uncertain employment, who may not know where the money for the next day's meal or next week's rent is coming from. In the UK, the fifth biggest economy in the world, people go hungry, feel alienated and dispossessed from the economy's riches. Class has been largely ignored in MOS for decades, but the debate between Spivak and Butler (2007) suggests ways of understanding the precarity of the dispossessed within the world's richer, as well as its poorer, economies.

I suspect MOS's engagement with Butler's work is in its infancy. Her continually evolving ideas offer a cornucopia of inspirations and insights for developing new theory and political practice.

Recommended reading

Original text by Judith Butler

Butler, J. (1990). *Gender Trouble*. London: Routledge, Chapman & Hall.
Butler, J. (1993). *Bodies That Matter*. New York: Routledge.

Butler's written work is dense, but her lectures and talks are lucid, comprehensible and often humorous. Rather than a written text I would recommend someone new to Butler should listen to her lectures and talks available online. After this, it is important to engage with *Gender Trouble* (1990) and *Bodies that Matter* (1993), but the prefaces or opening chapters of her later books often contain lucid summaries of the cumulative theory.

Key academic text

Lloyd, M. (1999). Performativity, parody, politics. *Theory, Culture & Society*, 16:2, 195–213 (For a sympathetic but critical approach to Butler's earlier work).

Accessible resource

Salih, S. (2002) *Judith Butler*. New York: Routledge. (In Routledge's *Critical Thinkers* series.)

Notes

1 Queer theory is a body of theory that explores how norms, particularly norms about sex, 'create' 'normative' and 'abject' identities. For a century, and still today in many parts of the world, heterosexuality is the normative identity, and homosexuality its abjected, controlled and oppressed other.
2 Of course I am referring here to what Butler (2004, p. 86) describes as 'bodily indicators [that] are the cultural means by which the sexed body is read. They are themselves bodily, and they operate as signs, so there is no easy way to distinguish between what is "materially" true, and what is "culturally" true about a sexed body'. That is, 'the body does not become sexually readable without those signs and ... those signs are irreducibly cultural and material at once'.

References

Alvesson, M. and Spicer, A. (2012). Critical leadership studies: The case for critical performativity. *Human Relations*, 65:3, 367–390.

Austin, J.L. (1962). *How to do things with words*. Oxford: Oxford University Press.

Borgerson, J. (2005). Judith Butler: On organizing subjectivities. *The Sociological Review*, 53:1_suppl, 63–79.

Butler, J. (1990). *Gender Trouble*. London: Routledge, Chapman & Hall.

Butler, J. (1993). *Bodies That Matter*. New York: Routledge.

Butler, J. (1997a). *The Psychic Life of Power*. Stanford, CA: Stanford University Press.

Butler, J. (1997b). *Excitable Speech: A Politics of the Performative*. New York: Routledge.

Butler, J. (2000). *Antigone's Claim*. New York: Columbia University Press.

Butler, J. (2004a). *Precarious Lives*. London: Verso.

Butler, J. (2004b). *Undoing Gender*. New York: Routledge.

Butler, J. (2005). *Giving an Account of Oneself*. New York: Fordham UP.

Butler, J. (2006). *Precarious Life: The Power of Mourning and Violence*. London: Verso.

Butler, J. (2009a). *Frames of War. When Is Life Grievable?* London: Verso.

Butler, J. (2009b). Performativity, precarity and sexual politics. *AIBR*, 4:3, i–xiii. Available at http://www.aibr.org/antropologia/04v03/criticos/040301b.pdf

Butler, J. (2010). Performative Agency. *Journal of Cultural Economy*, 3:2, 147–161.

Butler, J. (2015a). *Senses of the Subject*. New York: Fordham University Press.

Butler, J. (2015b). *Notes Towards a Performative Theory of Assembly*. Cambridge, MA: Harvard University Press.

Butler, J. and Athanasiou, A. (2013). *Dispossession: The Performative in the Political*. Cambridge: Polity Press.

Cabantous, L., Gond, J.P., Harding, N. and Learmonth, M. (2016). Critical essay: Reconsidering critical performativity. *Human Relations*, 69:2, 197–213.

Fleming, P. and Banerjee, S.B. (2016). When performativity fails: Implications for critical management studies. *Human Relations*, 69:2, 257–276.

Hancock, P. and Tyler, M. (2007). Un/doing gender and the aesthetics of organizational performance. *Gender, Work & Organization*, 14:6, 512–533.

Harding, N. (2013) *On Being at Work: The Social Construction of the Employee.* New York/London: Routledge.

Harding, N., Ford, J. and Lee, H. (2017). Towards a performative theory of resistance: Senior managers and revolting subject(ivitie)s. *Organization Studies*, 38:9, 1209–1232. (4*)

Kenny, K.M. (2010). Beyond ourselves: Passion and the dark side of identification in an ethical organization. *Human Relations*, 63:6, 857–873.

Learmonth, M., Harding, N., Gond, J.P. and Cabantous, L. (2016). Moving critical performativity forward. *Human Relations*, 69:2, 251–256.

Mumby, D.K. (2005). Theorizing resistance in organization studies: A dialectical approach. *Management Communication Quarterly*, 19:1, 19–44.

Ozturk, M.B. and Rumens, N. (2014). Gay male academics in UK business and management schools: Negotiating heteronormativities in everyday work life. *British Journal of Management*, 25:3, 503–517.

Parker, M. (2001). Fucking management: Queer, theory and reflexivity. *Ephemera* 1:1, 36–53.

Riach, K., Rumens, N. and Tyler, M. (2014). Un/doing chrononormativity: Negotiating ageing, gender and sexuality in organizational life. *Organization Studies*, 35:11, 1677–1698.

Riach, K., Rumens, N. and Tyler, M. (2016). Towards a Butlerian methodology: Undoing organizational performativity through anti-narrative research. *Human Relations*, 69:11, 2069–2089.

Rittenhofer, I. and Gatrell, C. (2012). Gender mainstreaming and employment in the European Union: A review and analysis of theoretical and policy literatures. *International Journal of Management Reviews*, 14, 201–216.

Spicer, A., Alvesson, M. and Kärreman, D. (2009). Critical performativity: The unfinished business of critical management studies. *Human Relations*, 62:4, 537–560.

Spicer, A., Alvesson, M. and Kärreman, D. (2016). Extending critical performativity. *Human Relations*, 69:2, 225–249.

Spivak, G.C. and Butler, J. (2007). *Who Sings the Nation-State?: Language, Politics, Belonging.* Kolkata: Seagull Books.

Tyler, M. and Cohen, L. (2010). Spaces that matter: Gender performativity and organizational space. *Organization Studies*, 31(2), 175–198.

Wickert, C. and Schaefer, S.M. (2015). Towards a progressive understanding of performativity in critical management studies. *Human Relations*, 68:1, 107–130.

Index

Note: Page numbers followed by "n" denote endnotes.

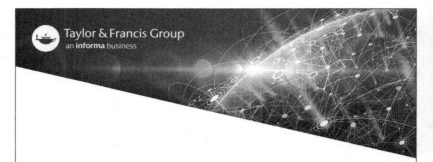

Printed in the United States
by Baker & Taylor Publisher Services